HOW
PORCUPINES
MAKE
LOVE II

Gi Style
Xmas
Vacation
1990

HOW PORCUPINES MAKE LOVE II

Teaching a Response-Centered Literature Curriculum

ALAN C. PURVES
STATE UNIVERISTY OF NEW YORK AT ALBANY

THERESA ROGERS
OHIO STATE UNIVERSITY

ANNA O. SOTER
OHIO STATE UNIVERSITY

Longman
New York & London

How Porcupines Make Love II:
Teaching a Response-Centered Literature Curriculum

Longman, 95 Church Street, White Plains, N.Y. 10601

Associated companies:
Longman Group Ltd., London
Longman Cheshire Pty., Melbourne
Longman Paul Pty., Auckland
Copp Clark Pitman, Toronto

Credits are listed on p. 186

Senior editor: Naomi Silverman
Production editor: Dee Amir Josephson
Text design adaptation: Dee Amir Josephson
Cover design: Susan J. Moore
Cover illustration/photo: Susan J. Moore
Text photos: Ted Purves
Production supervisor: Priscilla Taguer

Library of Congress Cataloging-in-Publication Data

Purves, Alan C., 1931–
How Porcupines Make Love II: Teaching a Response-Centered Literature
    Curriculum / by Alan C. Purves, Theresa Rogers, Anna Soter.
    p.   cm.
    Rev. ed. of: How porcupines make love. 1972.
    Includes bibliographical references.
    ISBN 0-8013-0382-6
    1. Literature—Study and teaching. I. Rogers, Theresa.
II. Soter, Anna O., 1946—.   III. Purves, Alan C., 1931— How
porcupines make love.   IV. Title
PN59.P84 1990
807—dc20   89-12969
                                                        CIP

ABCDEFGHIJ-MA-99   98   97   96   95   94   93   92   91   90

This book is dedicated to
our students, who are our other books

Contents

Preface

In 1988, fifteen years after the first edition of *How Porcupines Make Love*, two things happened. Alan Purves received a letter from Macmillan Publishing Co. (the fourth in a series of publishers that had acquired the title in a series of buy-outs and mergers) saying they were letting the book go out of print. Not since the original publisher, Xerox, had there been a publishing company where the editors had actually looked at the volume. One had listed it as Social Studies and another as Natural Science—so much for whimsy.

The second event was the appearance at Longman of Naomi Silverman, who asked Alan Purves about any new ideas. He replied that he thought literature instruction and curriculum might be getting a fresh go now that the cultural literacy people were around. She allowed as how Longman might be interested in a new volume, not a reprint. So the three authors, who had worked together on other projects over the years since all were at the University of Illinois, came up with a prospectus.

One thing we can say about this volume is that it has some of the same spirit as the earlier one, but it is tempered by our realization of the nature of the schools, students, teachers, principals, and parents. We have been teaching in every grade from K–12 and have been working with teachers in training and in-service teachers for a long time, and we know how dashing the reality of long days and weeks in unpainted classrooms can be. Yet we know that it is possible to keep up one's spirit and retain one's intellectual wits. We hope this text can help.

Writing this book required the collaboration of a number of people. We would like to thank the co-authors of the first edition of *How Procupines Make Love,* who generously turned over their rights and wished us well. Several are still teaching in the spirit of the original. We hope we have not violated their trust.

Among our colleagues, we would like to thank Frank Zidonis, Bertram Bruce, Merrlyn Cahill, Myra Molnar, Cecily O'Neill, Arthur Applebee, Noreen Benton, and Sean Walmsley. Linda Papa generously handled the permission correspondence. The manuscript was the loving work of Maribel Gray, who put up with our typographic idiosyncracies. Ted Purves helped with the art work. We are particularly grateful to our families who supported our efforts.

HOW PORCUPINES MAKE LOVE II

CHAPTER 1

Lighght and Lit

An anthology of the best writing from American literary magazines contained a poem titled "Lighght" by Aram Saroyan. The entire text of the poem is:

lighght

Television series and films often contain references to poets like T. S. Eliot, Emily Dickinson, or Langston Hughes.

Large-circulation magazines publish fiction that, ten years ago, would have appeared in an esoteric literary quarterly.

Serious fiction contains references to *The Cat in the Hat, Star Wars,* or Nancy Drew.

Advertisements contain frequent references to Shakespeare, folktales, and writers as diverse as Emily Brontë and Franz Kafka.

Readers of comic books are expected to be versed in molecular biology and Hindu mythology. Readers of poetry are expected to grasp allusions in the following poem to children's writers and comic books.

GOODBAT NIGHTMAN

God bless all policemen
and fighters of crime,
May thieves go to jail
for a very long time.

They've had a hard day
helping clean up the town,
Now they hang from the mantelpiece
both upside down.

A glass of warm blood
and then straight up the stairs,
Batman and Robin
are saying their prayers.

They've locked all the doors
and they've put out the bat,
Put on their batjamas
(They like doing that!)

They've filled their batwater-bottles
made their batbeds,
With two springy battresses
for sleepy batheads.

They're closing red eyes
and they're counting black sheep,
Batman and Robin
are falling asleep.

Roger McGough

Or grasp the full ramifications of this poem.

WAITING ON ELVIS, 1956

> This place up in Charlotte called Chuck's where I used to waitress and who
> came in one night but Elvis and some of his friends before his concert at
> the Arena, I was twenty-six married but still waiting tables and we got to
> joking around like you do, and he was fingering the lace edge of my slip
> where it showed below my hemline and I hadn't even seen it and I slapped
> at him a little saying, You sure are the one aren't you feeling my face
> burn but he was the kind of boy even meanness turned sweet in his mouth.

> Smiled at me and said, Yeah honey I guess I sure am.

Joyce Carol Oates

What's Been Happening to Literature and Our Culture?

Not so long ago it seemed easy to stratify our cultural life into highbrow,
middlebrow, and lowbrow; into mass-cult and mid-cult; or into popular and
private. Whatever the name given to the stratum and no matter exactly how
many strata were marked off, the notion of strata pervaded our thinking about
our cultural life. There were those who liked beer, baseball, and comics; and
those who liked espresso, polo, and Faulkner. Somewhere in the middle lay a
vast group that listened to light classics and belonged to the Book-of-the-
Month Club.

Into that stratified world, literature and literature-teaching fit very nicely.
The task was simple. Given a group of students who, teachers were sure,
preferred baseball and Batman to espresso and Faulkner, one simply had to
present them with the best of "classical culture" from Sophocles to Virginia
Woolf and trust that a larger percentage would end up subscribing to the
Book-of-the-Month. One of the ways of presenting the material was to sur-
round it with lots of biographical and historical information. Another way
was to stretch the works out on a dissecting table, so as to analyze their
patterns of imagery; search for ambiguities, puns, and paradoxes; and identify bits of synechdoche and metonymy. Still another way was to read what
some scholar had written about one of the works and then set out to make
the students come up with the scholar's interpretation. No matter the method;
what was important was the students' "covering" the great works. At no
point did the teacher question the status quo.

It was a nice plan—perhaps it did not fully accord with the way the
world was, but it was a nice simple plan. To be sure, serious writers had
long been working for the film companies, poets in advertising agencies, and
Marianne Moore liked baseball, but these must have been "aberrations."

Teachers did not mention the fact that William Faulkner had worked in
Hollywood or H. L. Mencken had long attacked the pompous notions of

what culture was, or that *The New Yorker* and *Esquire* had long sought to bring together the various facets of American culture. They didn't notice that real men ate quiche and drank espresso.

For many teachers, what was happening in the world of book and magazine publishing or the world of films had nothing to do with literature classes. Then a number of things came along to upset their organized world.

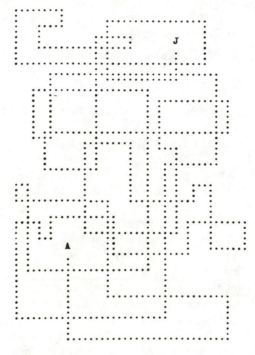

Estrangement

Figure 1.2A and 1.2B. One of these appeared in a volume of poetry; the other in *Mad* magazine.

Television, mass enrollment in high schools and colleges, the surges in the circulation of the "mid-cult" magazines, and the incorporation of good writing and pornographic pictures within a single cover. Then students turned into their own culture. The culture of rock, punk, heavy metal, graffiti, and T-shirts—not to mention shopping malls. This culture moved up and became fashionable and trendy. It's hard to tell who's highbrow and who's lowbrow.

For good or bad, serious artists were taking popular culture seriously. For good or bad, the understatements of the high culture became a part of the advertising world and thus a part of everybody's culture. For good or bad, writers became interested in how their books looked. For good or bad, photographers and cinematographers worked with writers, or, like photographer Gordon Parks, wrote themselves.

Another aspect of this change is the rise into deserved prominence of writers who had long been considered oddities. "Negro writer," "Jewish writer," "lady writer" were terms that helped people look down on Richard Wright, Irwin Shaw, or Willa Cather. Such terms cannot be used condescendingly today.

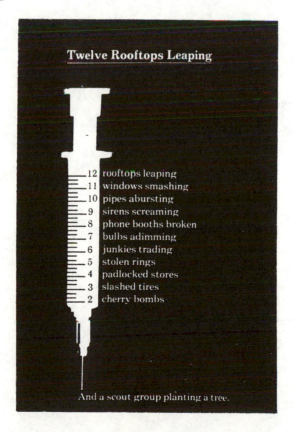

Twelve Rooftops Leaping

12 rooftops leaping
11 windows smashing
10 pipes abursting
9 sirens screaming
8 phone booths broken
7 bulbs adimming
6 junkies trading
5 stolen rings
4 padlocked stores
3 slashed tires
2 cherry bombs

And a scout group planting a tree.

Everything Got Mixed Up Even More than It Had Been

We now have such a cross-fertilization between "high" and "low" culture in our writing that to use such a distinction to put down a writer doesn't make much sense (good and bad, yes; but high and low, no).

We now have a mingling of writing and the graphic arts (and the aural arts) into a mélange of media. Literature refuses to rest securely in 10-point type on the page. Literature includes both scripted and improvised theater, film, television drama, videotext, performance art, and ancient ritual.

Much of it demands to be looked at, to be heard, to be read all at once. It demands to be taken as fun. Fun that had its serious moments, but fun nevertheless. Eve Merriam can place a poem of social protest in the setting of a Christmas carol.

It demands that we enjoy it and feel its power.

It demands that we respond to it creatively.

A HELPING HAND

We gave a helping hand to grass—
    and it turned into corn.
We gave a helping hand to fire—
    and it turned into a rocket.
Hesitatingly,
cautiously,
we give a helping hand
to people,
to some people. . .

Miroslav Holub

PINEAPPLE PLAY

Narrator
In a poem you make your point with pineapples.
(PINEAPPLES fly onto stage from all directions.)

Spy
And it would be nice to have a spy going in and out.

End

Ruth Krauss

Literature demands to be taken naturally:

> Most of all I like writing for people untouched by poetry, for instance, for those who do not even know that it should be at all for them. I would like them to read poems as naturally as they read the papers, or go up to a football game. Not to consider it as anything more difficult, or effeminate, or praiseworthy

writes the Czech biologist-poet Miroslav Holub.

Kenneth Koch has shown that children in the primary grades can write good poems by any standard.

Literature demands even more strongly than ever before that the traditional barriers between genres be looked at as inconsequential, that such classification fails because it does not provide useful distinctions. Tom Wolfe writes essays that resemble fiction. Docudramas demand to be witnessed as literature. Poems read like essays and essays like poems. Ads pose as theater.

Borges and I

The other one, the one called Borges, is the one things happen to. I walk through the streets of Buenos Aires and stop for a moment, perhaps mechanically now, to look at the arch of an entrance hall and the grillwork on the gate; I know of Borges from the mail and see his name on a list of professors or in a biographical dictionary. I like hourglasses, maps, eighteenth-century typography, the taste of coffee and the prose of Stevenson; he shares these preferences, but in a vain way that turns them into the attributes of an actor. It would be an exaggeration to say that ours is a hostile relationship; I live, let myself go on living, so that Borges may contrive his literature, and this literature justifies me. It is no effort for me to confess that he has achieved some valid pages, but those pages cannot save me, perhaps because what is good belongs to no one, not even to him, but rather to the language and to tradition. Besides, I am destined to perish, definitively, and only some instant of myself can survive in him. Little by little, I am giving over everything to him, though I am quite aware of his perverse custom of falsifying and magnifying things. Spinoza knew that all things long to persist in their being; the stone eternally wants to be a stone and the tiger a tiger. I shall remain in Borges, not in myself (if it is true that I am someone), but I recognize myself less in his books than in many others or in the laborious strumming of a guitar. Years ago I tried to free myself from him and went from the mythologies of the suburbs to the games with time and infinity, but those games belong to Borges now and I shall have to imagine other things. Thus my life is a flight and I lose everything and everything belongs to oblivion, or to him.

I do not know which of us has written this page.

Jorge Luis Borges
Translated by J. E. I.

Yet literature, like all art, demands to be taken seriously: When you make a poem you merely speak or write the language of every day, capturing as many bonuses as possible and economizing on losses; that is, you come awake to what always goes on in language, and you use it to the limit of your ability and your power of attention at the moment. You always fail, to some extent, since the opportunities are infinite—but think of the extent of your failure in ordinary conversation! Poetry bears the brunt, though; for in trying for the best it calls attention to its vivid failures.

William Stafford

It even demands that the traditional language barriers be broken. Good translations of poets abound. Fiction and drama have become virtually international: witness the awarding of a National Book Award to a Brazilian novel; witness the many national touring companies of major plays; witness the polyglot or monoglot (depending on how you look at it) cinema, with actors and directors from all over the world converging in a film.

It has long demanded not to be censored and has taken everything for its province: Hamlet, homosexuality, sadism, smog, masturbation, the flag, AIDS, Black Masses, computers, and race. Revolution has been the topic of poems printed in the more staid journals.

"Literature," once the private preserve of the cultivated happy few, has become anarchic, joyful, and vital.

In fact, the term *literature* hardly applies to this congeries of writing, graphics, sound, music, film, and tape.

HOW EVERYTHING HAPPENS[1]
(BASED ON A STUDY OF THE WAVE)

```
                                                                    happen.
                                                          to
                                                      up
                                          stacking
                                    is
                       something
When nothing is happening
When it happens
                  something
                              pulls
                                    back
                                          not
                                             to
                                                happen.
When                                         has happened.
        pulling back              stacking up
                       happens
             has happened                                      stacks up.
When it                    something                  nothing
                                      pulls back while
Then nothing is happening.
                                           happens.
                                      and
                          forward
                    pushes
                up
            stacks
        something
Then
```

---

[1]May Swenson, "The Watch," copyright © 1965; "How Everything Happens (Based on a Study of the Wave)," copyright © 1969; Poem by May Swenson, reprinted by permission of the author.

Forms have broken down; the regularity of print has been challenged; taboos of subject matter have shifted; but mere anarchy is not loosed upon the world. Literature is undergoing one of its perennial shifts whereby every convention is being tested and used as the springboard for trying out new modes of expression.

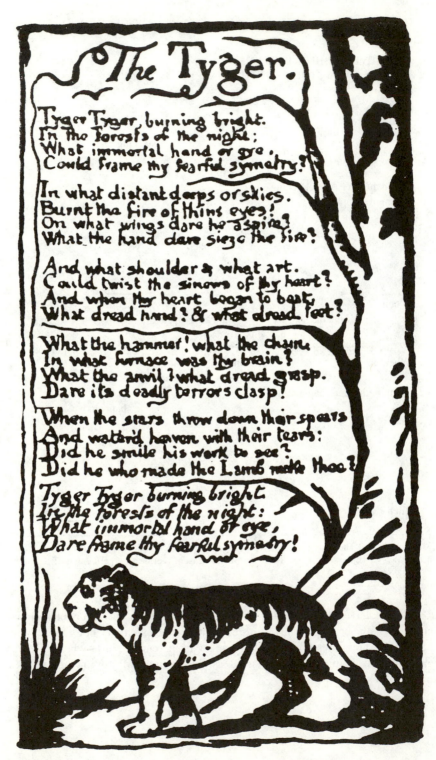

The Tyger.

Tyger Tyger, burning bright.
In the forests of the night;
What immortal hand or eye,
Could frame thy fearful symmetry?

In what distant deeps or skies.
Burnt the fire of thine eyes!
On what wings dare he aspire?
What the hand dare sieze the fire?

And what shoulder & what art.
Could twist the sinows of thy heart?
And when thy heart began to beat,
What dread hand? & what dread foot?

What the hammer! what the chain.
In what furnace was thy brain?
What the anvil? what dread grasp.
Dare its deadly terrors clasp!

When the stars throw down their spears
And water'd heaven with their tears:
Did he smile his work to see?
Did he who made the Lamb make thee?

Tyger Tyger burning bright.
In the forests of the night:
What immortal hand or eye,
Dare frame thy fearful symmetry!

Where Have the Old Values Gone?

It depends on what values you mean. If it is the value of the able expression of a meaningful experience, that value has remained. If it is the "value" of a classic being a classic just because someone thought it was a classic and everyone had to worship it as a classic, that value has faded away.

Value has remained, but values and evaluators and the literary stock market have come under increasing attack. The criteria by which people judge pieces of writing have been challenged. Who says a work must end with a period, must have a single static form, must accord to the "rules" of a genre, must deal with the niceties, must be written by one person, or even by a person? Who says great literature must always be about humanity's deepest thought or must be taken seriously? Who says that a work must have a single meaning? Who says a work must use words?

All of these questions are matters of taste, and taste is subject to change.

Values have remained, but they are continually tested and challenged by new creations. One value that has remained is the value of pleasure. Literature seeks to please the person who made it and the person who attends to it. Pleasure is not the same as laughter, but is a sense that what is written is as it should be.

Has This Bursting of the Bonds of Convention, Genre, Standards Never Happened Before?

Of course it has. It happened when the Elizabethans played havoc with dramatic form and with the Italian sonnet. It happened when opera introduced the mixing of media. It happened with the novel in the eighteenth century. It happened with poetry in almost every generation. Writers have continually sought to "make it new," to modify the conventions set by their predecessors and to forge their own forms, themes, combinations of words, of media, of ideas. Often they have failed; often they have succeeded.

Today's writers are no different, save that they have more traditions to play against, more gadgets to play with, more areas of information to assimilate into their writing, and—most important of all—a larger literate audience. They are no longer dependent upon a small number of publishers. With a computer and a laser printer they can produce their own books.

What makes the plethora of writings, forms, themes, mixtures, seem inchoate to many teachers of English is that literary education has gotten itself all mixed up with writers and what they do. A couple of hundred years ago, the schools taught Latin and Greek. English and American literature were not part of the school or college curriculum (save for a few excerpts that were used to teach people how to read). Writers wrote.

When education became the province of all, Latin and Greek literature were replaced by English literature, but it was the English literature of the sixteenth, seventeenth, and eighteenth centuries. In the universities this literature was studied historically, connected with the development of the language and with the moral and political life of the times in which it was written. In the high schools, works were read for their beauty of expression and their purity of thought—read, that is, as models of ethics and style. Writers went on writing.

Magpielike Chaucer borrowed plots, themes, lines from contemporary writers as well as from the "classics." He also had fun poking holes in literary conventions.

So did Shakespeare:

My mistress' eyes are nothing like the sun,
Coral is far more red than her lips' red.
If snow be white, why then her breasts are dun,
If hairs be wires, black wires grow in her head.
I have seen roses damasked, red and white,
But no such roses see I in her cheeks.
And in some perfumes is there more delight
Than in the breath that from my mistress reeks.
I love to hear her speak, yet well I know
That music hath a far more pleasing sound.
I grant I never saw a goddess go,
My mistress, when she walk, treads on the ground.
    And yet, by heaven, I think my love as rare
    As any she belied with false compare.

Sonnet 130

Thomas Carlyle was so unsatisfied with the form of the philosophical thesis that he invented a German writer and an editor to present his ideas. The result was *Sartor Resartus*. Karl Marx imitated him and started a revolution.

When *Moby Dick* came out, critics condemned it for not fitting any of their literary categories.

Ambrose Bierce found that one of the most congenial forms for him was the "dictionary." In his *Devil's Dictionary*, he defines a critic:

CRITIC, n. A person who boasts himself hard to please because nobody tries to please him.

There is a land of pure delight,
Beyond the Jordan's flood,
Where saints, apparelled all in white,
Fling back the critic's mud.

And as he legs it through the skies,
His pelt a sable hue,
He sorrows sore to recognize
The missiles that he threw.

                              Orrin Goof

During the course of this century, the university study of literature has attained the proportions of a big business. Pieces of writing have acquired barnacles of articles, books, and dissertations, with definitive editions, annotated editions, scholarly editions, variorum editions; with examinations of structure, imagery, and metaphor; with interpretations political, social, psychological, aesthetic, and moral; with computerized concordances and bibliographies of bibliographies. Shakespeare, needless to say, has become the most encrusted. Students who want to know all that has been said about *Hamlet* would have to spend their lifetimes reading that body of texts alone.

Criticism has become such a growth industry it produced a spin-off— theory. That's bigger than scholarship today.

In the schools, this industry has shown itself in the many curriculum guides and teaching aides that accompany each text, in the revolving book racks of drugstores, which are often filled not with novels, poems, plays, and nonfiction, but with master outlines and study guides to the great works. The accumulation of knowledge and secondhand opinions about what writers have written has superseded the reading and enjoying of what they have written. Literary study, even in the junior high school, is a very serious business, wherein meanings, structures, ambiguities, and backgrounds take the place of reading, responding, and enjoying. All of this study requires that literature be seen as a fixed entity, that the text exist as data, that the definitions of *poem, irony, point of view, metaphor* be fixed so that it can be taught to children the way multiplication tables and the parts of speech are taught to children. And writers go on writing.

Writers don't seem to pay too much attention to what goes on in school. Have they forgotten what they have been taught? Or is it that they, like so many of their predecessors, have realized that literature methodized becomes a literature that stagnates?

Don't be fooled into thinking that literary scholarship is valueless. On the contrary, critical commentary, historical study, textual editing, bibliographical enterprise, even theory are all valuable, particularly to teachers, not because they give us the truth that they purport to give us, but because they allow us to see the ways in which people have responded to pieces of writing. They have become a testimony to the power of the mind to read, and to construct and test hypotheses about what it reads. They form a testimony to the ability of people to organize and build structures out of a collocation of objects that might be considered unique were it not for our structure-building capacities.

Like the scientists' elaborate organization of natural phenomena, like the historians' network connecting human events and actions, like the psychologists' theories of human behavior, the literary scholars' web of biographical, historical, generic, structural, archetypal, and rhetorical connections between poem and poem, between play and play, between novel and essay is a triumph. But it is not the same thing as works it deals with, just as science is not nature, and history is not human events.

Sing, goddess, the anger of Peleus' son Achilleus
and its devastation, which put pains thousandfold upon the Achaians,
hurled in their multitudes to the house of Hades strong souls. . .
of heroes, but gave their bodies to be the delicate feasting
of dogs. . . .

What happens to a dream deferred?

The curfew tolls the knell of parting day,
The lowing herd wind slowly o'er the lea,
The ploughman homeward plods his weary way,
And leaves the world to darkness and to me.

When shall we three meet again?
in thunder, lightning, or in rain. . . .

I am an invisible man.

They told me, Heraclitus, they told me you were dead. . . .

It is a truth universally acknowledged, that a single man in possession
of a good fortune must be in want of a wife.

Let us go then, you and I,
When the evening is spread out against the sky. . . .

"You, Tom!"

By and by
God caught his eye. . . .

Call me Ishmael.

Hope is a thing with feathers

I too dislike it.

I'm lighting out for the territory.

Literature is . . . but *literature* isn't there is perhaps no such thing as *literature*. As far as general education is concerned there are poems, and plays, and stories, and the Bible, and myths, and cartoons, and jokes, but *literature?* Literature is an abstraction, a network. For different people, literature is different networks. For some it is all the information about authors and publishers and audiences; just the way for some the Beatles were everything about Paul, Ringo, George, and John but their music. For some it is an elaborate code set forth to trap the unwary reader who must continually read between the lines. For some it is an infinite series of changes upon a few themes. For some it is a verbal manifestation of the totality of the human psyche—a model of the human.

Perhaps the broadest definition is one that states: It is a vast assortment of verbal (usually) utterances, each of which comes from some writer, who has a voice; and each of which in itself has some order. It includes Calvin and Hobbes and the *Divine Comedy*. Pieces of literature are such as to rouse a response—a sense of knowing, a sense of feeling, a sense of moving—in me. When these senses coalesce I have a kind of pleasure, a sense of the fitness of things. Out of having read what I've read, I construct a theory—a theory building upon the nature of language and upon the nature of the mind and upon the meeting of language and mind in what I would call response.

But If What You Have Said Is True, Then Your Definition of Literature Doesn't Matter? Does It?

Of Course Not.

Well, Then, What About Literature Courses?

At the center of the curriculum are *not* the works of literature, those collections of words in print or in sound wave, or the individual psyche with its neurological movements and its constantly changing psychological states and constantly modifying sets of images and concepts. . .

but

all those lines connecting the two. The mind as it meets the book. The response. That is the center of a curriculum in literature. Treat those lines carefully, or the book will become dead and the mind will retreat into itself. But treat those lines and you will have a response-centered curriculum.

Column A		Column B
sounds		feelings
syllables		memories
typefaces		concepts
words		stereotypes
phrases		word associations
images		sound associations
metaphors	Take at	word meanings
logical relationships	least one	favorite rhythms
characters	term	syntactic
actions	from	ideas about people
symbols	Column A	ideas about society
settings	and at	ideas about nature
paragraphs	least one	ideas about abstractions
meters	from	previous works read
rhythms	Column B.	political beliefs
figures of speech	Connect	religious beliefs
dialogue	each to	criteria about form
description	every other	subconscious desires
narration	and enjoy	moral censor
action	your literary	ego drive
pictures	theory.	psychological state
tones		aesthetic criteria
perspectives		sense of what is significant
moods		theory of literature
poems		philosophy of life. . . .
plays		
stories		
epics. . . .		

CHAPTER 2

Those Kids—Readers, Writers, Listeners, Mall Rats

They come in all shapes, hair colors and styles, peachy skin and fuzz, short and tall. At thirteen they are at the threshold of (for them) an unmapped terrain even though millions of us before them have passed the same way. They know nothing and yet everything. Filled with exuberance in the morning and dashed to the floor by the afternoon, they are puzzling, frustrating, challenging and, in their own way, refreshingly wonderful.

Some still have the innocence of childhood with them but it's fast becoming tempered by "knowledge." Some didn't have that innocence in the first place—life had already begun its lessons from birth. But although we talk about this group of people as one, adolescents are not one amorphous group; they are not totally molded yet by the social system and its instrument—school.

Why should we bother to write a chapter about them? After all, they're a recognizable age group, we've heard a great deal about them, and they are "students" in secondary school. We try to label them as one homogeneous group. In many respects they share characteristics, but while the socializing process of schooling has usually done a fairly good job in creating them as an identifiable group, individual characteristics possibly create even more conflicts (inner, if not outer) than they did in the days of childhood. They now have confidence that was generally less overt before, to challenge the authority they had earlier accepted. They have a need, now, to discover "themselves" among the social glob. Because they are highly critical of themselves they are equally critical of others (even if silently—read their journals). While in the process of separating self from self and self from others, they appear to have an even greater need than in childhood of identification within a group. Many observers of high schools have noted that students value their school friendships and social relationships more than they do their school subjects and teachers.

Back to our question—why bother to bring up the characteristics of adolescence in the context of discussing literature? There are three compelling reasons for doing so.

First, there is the question of what literary selections to present to them, if we want to keep their interests in mind. Second, there is the question of how we best engage them in literary discussion and succeed in bringing about that often elusive goal of having them develop a love and appreciation of literature (one of the most frequently stated aims of literature curricula though often the least achieved). Third, they know a great deal more than we allow them to tell us. The *way* we teach literature, therefore, is, perhaps, even more important than *what* we teach.

Selection and relevance are important components in the literature curriculum. However, if we close off what adolescents can say and write in response to literature through too much "telling" and too little "doing" on their part, and through too much narrow questioning not so much about the literature itself but about how we analyze it, we rarely, if ever, discover the richness and perceptiveness of their literary understanding. We simply make them inarticulate and dependent on others to read for them.

Curricular Goals and the Mall Rats

Ask aspiring teachers of English their aims in teaching literature and most say "I want my students to *love* literature." Then follows a litany of other objectives related to understanding literature, appreciating it, comprehending it, being able to identify literary elements.

But the primary aim is related to getting "them" to love literature (presumably just as we English teachers love it). Yet, we approach that objective from an adult's perspective. Proof of the pudding? Ask another question: "How do you intend to teach your literature classes?" A survey of 230 aspiring teachers in a secondary English certification program revealed a less than unanimous response to this question. Surprisingly few suggested that the literature chosen for study should be relevant to the adolescent student. Surprisingly few suggested extensive choice made by the student. Prodding them still further, we find an assumption that reflects our own experiences rather than that of the contemporary adolescent student: "I" love literature and "I" managed to "get hooked on it"—and somehow so will they. "I" will help them get there. The teacher is still the director and the student is still "the student"—a generic breed that appears to have lost its individual identities.

Perhaps this worked (up to a point) some twenty years ago and perhaps it worked even ten years ago. The current generation of aspiring teachers still has one foot that was born in a more book-oriented background. And, there seem to be fewer and fewer of these hardy survivors. But the current teenager comes to us with stiffer competition—a media world far more immediately accessible than any book can offer; far more immediately engaging than reading, despite our protests. Yes, their need to do well, to get those grades up, still helps us in our task of promoting good literature, but we have also seen many classrooms where the number of those "really there" is hardly encouraging.

A Vignette

Not too long ago one of us was observing a student-teacher in an eleventh-grade literature classroom in a large suburban high school. The story being discussed was Hawthorne's "Dr. Heidegger's Experiment," which is about an elderly scientist and his discovery of a youth-reviving elixir. He brings together three now octogenarian rivals and the former object of their passion—a still vain fading beauty. He offers them the elixir and for a brief half hour they are youthful again. However, instead of applying the lessons gained throughout years of disappointment and bitterness they repeat the errors spawned by greed, pride, and vanity and ultimately destroy the elixir and their chance to have eternal youth and beauty. The story was contained in a typical literature high school anthology appended with questions.

The teacher "taught" the story, explaining all she knew about the author and his assumed intentions. Questions were fielded to the class but the majority were visibly switched off—after all, they quickly realized that the questions would be answered by the teacher, keen to share what she knew. So they doodled, lounged, dozed, and wriggled, but on the surface of it appeared to be "there" insofar as they didn't cause discipline problems. But there was one exception. A long-haired 16-year-old, leather-jacketed, ear-ringed, and lightly moustached, raised his hand brightly for almost every question. He sat in the front row near the door and was remarkably engaged. He also knew "the answers."

This student was intriguing. He was obviously sharp and took trouble to extend his answers so that they weren't just one-line responses. Reference to the text was made, elaborations given—a teacher's dream student. One could sense that he was also a leader in the class and thus received the passive cooperation of the other students. The lesson ended with most of it having been a monologue occasionally interspersed by the dialogue with this student. The regular literature teacher confirmed that the student was indeed bright and a leader in the class. The student had heard that the student-teacher was to be "graded" that day and put on what he perceived as a wonderful performance for her sake.

The student-teacher is a novice, and we hope that the experiences at the school and others later will lead her to realize that teaching doesn't necessarily mean learning nor does it mean automatic engagement on the part of the students. What was impressive in that visit was the generosity of spirit in these kids, generally bored as they were, and their ability to help someone out—someone who hadn't been their most popular person for the previous quarter.

Generally, teachers regard adolescents beyond grade seven as a group to be controlled; they view classrooms as battlefields on which the teacher has to win and the students' cooperation is certainly not to be taken for granted. We suspect that much of this perception is rightly there—many students, including English majors, see their English classes in high school as deadly dull and confusing. English is a riddle they never really cracked. They survived by finding out what the teacher wanted and delivering it as best they could. Sitting in classrooms where the teacher does most of the work (i.e., talking, reading, sometimes even writing if we include blackboard work) generates isolation and apathy. Adolescents are not without energy; physically, emotionally, and intellectually they hum outside the classroom. Much of the energy may be misdirected according to adult eyes, but quashing it appears to generate an enormous waste of potential.

Another Vignette

Another teacher we recently observed in an eighth-grade classroom had tapped the hum. It wasn't a literature classroom but a spin-off writing workshop where the students were working with each other on a newspaper to be produced some weeks to come. They talked with each other; some were busy writing drafts of their contributions; others were reviewing pieces already written and discussing them with the relevant writers. Perhaps there were kids in there who chatted about things other than the newspaper, but we'd be living in fantasy if we thought that sort of thing didn't go on in the "regular" classroom. Remember all those notes we used to write to each other while keeping track of the teacher's questioning and talking?

The enormous energy of adolescence can be drawn on for engaging students through active participation in the literature classroom. Many current high school classrooms are mini-versions of college classrooms. Students sit and make notes while teachers largely lecture. As we've already stated, this may work for adult students, but many high school classroom observations indicate that it is hardly productive nor is it a way of "hooking" students to good literature.

Kids and Books

What is it that "hooks" kids to books? Why is it that some of us do and some of us don't? These questions still perplex educational researchers who are more interested in research on "reading skills." Increasingly, such researchers are finding evidence that those who become literate do so for a number of reasons that go far beyond skills levels and even "effective teaching."

Among such reasons are the role of background knowledge of what we read and (already having) the kind of knowledge that books assume we have in order to make sense of them. Another reason lies in the literacy-rich environments that produce children who read before they come to school and provide a continuous support for ongoing reading throughout school.

So far, however, we really haven't tackled the delicate question of "relevance" of materials in the school context. One of the reasons why we haven't done so, we suspect, is that this nudges at the door of the possibly unthinkable—we may find that the literature we think *all* students should be able to read and should love to read (i.e., "the classics") is not of any particular relevance to them. If we find this to be an answer, what do we do then?

But thinking about this dilemma leads us to one of the interesting facts about literature that appears to be overlooked by the "relevancy" argument and which all young children, at least, have inadvertently provided powerful argument for: that the world of imaginative discourse (i.e., literature) can help us leap across domains that we find unthinkable in the skills-based world. If this were not so, how can young children love fantasy? If this were not so, how is it that science fiction can even survive? If this were not so, how can young adolescent readers (and even older ones) continue to love stories of the romantic kind where the tall, dark, and handsome man can still be the one who emerges when all seems lost to rescue the poor maiden from a romantic "death"?

It seems that when we pick up a literary book we already accept that "the unreal" is possible; that we suspend our disbelief just as Wordsworth said we must; that we can engage in flights of fancy and become really involved in ways that elude us with nonfictional reading. The same students who have trouble with a geography text don't quail before exploring the fantastic world of Tolkien! We won't discuss why in this chapter since it is an issue covered elsewhere in this book. At least one of the answers lies in the nature of literature as a distinct genre that sets it apart from fact-based genres as well as the response we have to it, from other kinds of reading we do whether willingly or unwillingly.

Despite what we have just said, however, the relevance issue is not so easily dismissed. At least one of us has tried to introduce the wonders of *Wind in the Willows* to an eighth-grade class and largely been defeated only to turn to a class-based choice—a little novel entitled *Thursday*, aimed at the adolescent reader aged about fourteen, with a 14-year-old antihero and a heroine who brings the antihero to his senses. They loved that! Yet we have also taught ninth graders who were spellbound by hearing and reading Shakespeare's *King Lear*, who were so enthralled during the last act that we could, literally, hear a pin drop, and who intuitively understood the enormity of the pain experienced by Lear as he carried Cordelia from the dungeon.

Selection is a significant factor in helping adolescents (and any reader) become engaged in what they read. To help us determine on what basis such selections could be made, we suggest considering the nature of adolescence— not in terms of the limits this age group imposes but in terms of the scope it offers.

Who Is "The Adolescent"?

What is the identity of the high school student? Can we even really talk about "the adolescent"? Any seasoned secondary teacher will talk about seventh graders still being fresh and enthusiastic and pliable; eighth graders as unpredictable and yet still delightfully spontaneous, and, yes, still interested in "learning"; then there are *those* ninth graders—ugh! Increasingly incomprehensible, intractable, bored, moody, dominated by hormones. Somehow the rigors of test-taking and college-bound making-it take care of the tenth to twelfth graders, for we tend not to hear of them in terms of their characters, their development, their inability to sit still quite so frequently. They are simply swallowed up in the need to do well and to get on in the grade grind. They have learned to be passive students not active readers.

Phases of adolescent development are reasonably well covered in educational psychology. We don't intend to go over the same ground in this chapter. We can, however, bring to the literature classroom some of the findings of that research and integrate it with such things as literary selection, the question of relevance, and what we can expect in literary understanding and appreciation.

Although our discussion is limited to the notion of "adolescent" we will try to stress the range of that age group in terms of a developmental continuum. A twelfth grader is not an eighth grader and, consequently, suggestions for selection, and our understanding of what we can expect of students' ability to appreciate literary qualities in the literature they read, will be modified by the specific period of adolescence we are discussing at any particular point.

Personal/Social Development

> But Mole stood still a moment, held in thought. As one wakened suddenly from a beautiful dream, who struggles to recall it, and can recapture nothing but a dim sense of the beauty of it, the beauty! Till that, too, fades away in its turn, and the dreamer bitterly accepts the hard, cold waking and all its penalties; so Mole, after struggling with his memory for a brief space, shook his head sadly and followed the Rat.
>
> Kenneth Grahame, *Wind in the Willows*

In her book *In the Middle,* Nancie Atwell dedicates a chapter to the characteristics of adolescents. Mole's intimations of "the cold hard world" of reality are part of the adolescent's ability to see patterns and significances in what were once just isolated events. Writers of contemporary adolescent literature also depict this movement from the relatively untroubled world of childhood into adulthood, as can be seen in the following extracts:

> "Meg, don't you think you'd make a better adjustment to life if you faced facts?"
>
> "I do face facts," Meg said. "They're lots easier to face than people, I can tell you."
>
> Madeleine L'Engle, *A Wrinkle in Time*

or

> . . . . She was in a different line and a few feet behind, and as she looked at the back of his head she was overwhelmed by the fact that at that very moment she was creating her own past. To let Dennis go his way and for her to go her own without even saying a word would be a memory she'd have to have for the rest of her life. It seemed as if it was something Liz should have known, and Sean. They should have known what they were risking. The present becomes the past, and it continues inside you.
>
> Paul Zindel, *My Darling, My Hamburger*

And there would be many examples from Dickens and other "classical writers" that attest to the same development in their heroes, sometimes even younger than adolescents. As social beings, adolescents often question adult authority while at the same time wishing to figure out adult reality:

> I began to realize that my coffee trips were futile—they only brought temporary relief whereas these people needed something more permanent with more individual care and attention. But the needs of these outcasts were insufficiently met or even understood by the public. To give them practical help needed money, time and professional skills. Of which I had none. My own inadequacy to assist them haunted me, so I went in search of others who felt the same. I found people kind and sympathetic, but not prepared to stick their necks out and become involved. What was so frustrating was that most of the objections were reasonable.
>
> Sally Trench, *Bury Me in My Boots*

One problem that adolescents appear to experience (though adults aren't immune to it) that makes adult reality confusing at times is actually an outcome of their new ability to see shades of gray amidst the black-and-white world of childhood. An adolescent has already had time and experience to discover, for example, that when something is promised it doesn't necessarily eventuate immediately, and sometimes, it may never do so. Another reality to be faced is an awareness that ethics and morality may, in fact, be relative and not absolute. Adults get away with things. Adults are inconsistent and imperfect even though they expect children not to be so and their kids know it:

> . . . There was a rule at Lark Creek, more important than anything Mr. Turner made up and fussed about. That was the rule that you never mixed up troubles at home with life at school.
> When parents were poor or ignorant or mean, or even just didn't believe in having a TV set, it was up to their kids to protect them.
>
> Katherine Paterson, *Bridge to Terabithia*

In both the classics and contemporary adolescent literature, we can find examples of the realities that adolescents begin to reflect on as part of adult life—for example, "the unfair," the "hard to explain."

Another Vignette

The scene: A dramatization of several stories by Poe and other writers, among them Shirley Jackson's "The Lottery." In a theater seating over a thousand students, all eighth and ninth graders, not a sound could be heard during the performance. Between performances there had been a good deal of wriggling and talking. "The Lottery" is not a story written for or about adolescents. It tells of the brutality of ritualized control over a small rural community, the fate of individuals in it from infancy to old age controlled by a mindless casting of lots. It did not escape this audience of 14- and 15-year-olds.

One of the harder lessons to be faced by the emerging adult is isolation from peers. The isolation may be a consequence of difference (interpreted as "oddness" by the peers) or a consequence of making a moral or ethical choice at a significant price. A number of classical novels and contemporary adolescent novels deal with this issue (without happy endings), offering an opportunity for this age group to explore how they would face such situations themselves. For example, in Dickens' *Great Expectations*, we can see three parallel situations in which characters are isolated: Pip, the orphan; Magwitch, the convict; and Miss Havisham, the embittered, jilted old woman. The novel focuses on Pip's personal and moral/ethical development against the backdrop of his illusions about wealth and what it represents. His great moments come when he can genuinely love the social outcast, Magwitch, and accept that it was this man who was responsible for Pip having had "great expectations." Pip's struggles to accept the truth of the origin of his temporary fortune and his ability to see real worth vs. the glitter that had formerly blinded him are representative of the growth we must all make:

> But I must say more. Dear Joe, I hope you will have children to love, and that some little fellow will sit in this chimney corner of a winter night, who may remind you of another little fellow gone out of it forever. Don't tell him, Joe, that I was thankless; don't tell him, Biddy, that I was ungenerous and unjust; only tell him that I honoured you both, because you were both so good and true, and that, as your child, I said it would be natural to him to grow up a better man than I did.
>
> Dickens, *Great Expectations*

Another example generating empathy among adolescent readers is found in Charlotte Brontë's *Jane Eyre*. Jane has just arrived at Lowood and in the assembly called by Mr. Brocklehurst, director of that awesome institution, breaks her slate. She realizes that she will not be able to escape his attention and that she must finally face the trial of his judgments on her:

> A pause—in which I began to steady the palsy of my nerves, and to feel that the Rubicon had passed and that the trial, no longer to be avoided, must be finally sustained.
>
> Charlotte Brontë, *Jane Eyre*

Adolescents we have known and taught do empathize with these heroes and heroines whose isolation and exclusion, whose trials and challenges, are still essentially those of the contemporary teenager. A compelling contemporary example is Robert Cormier's *The Chocolate War* in which the young hero, Jerry, faces death largely because he didn't go along with the crowd:

> Jerry raised himself toward the voice, needing to answer it. He had to answer. But he kept his eyes shut, as if he could keep a lid on the pain that way. But it was more than pain that caused an urgency in him. The pain had become the nature of his existence but this other thing weighed on him, a terrible burden. What other thing? The knowledge, the knowledge: what he had discovered. Funny, how his mind was clear suddenly, apart from his body, floating above his body, floating above the pain.
>
> Robert Cormier, *The Chocolate War*

Although Jerry's pain is a consequence of what other boys his own age have done, the knowledge is that first sign of understanding of the significance of events. Similarly, in John Neufeld's *Lisa, Bright and Dark*, the students who attempt to help a fellow 16-year-old cope with her developing mania come to realize that they cannot hope to expect cooperation and help from the adults closest to her—her parents and school authorities—all of whom turn a blind eye on the situation. The disbelief eventually becomes the foundation not only for disillusionment with the adults, but also understanding of what makes them tick.

Both "the classics" and contemporary adolescent fiction offer a wide variety of selections that explore issues very relevant to this age group. Some of these we've already explored. Other issues or problems related to adolescence include the preoccupation with peers, wide swings of mood and intense passions, feelings of isolation, relativity. But it needn't all be grim, and heroes and heroines may also be admired for achieving greatness.

We've already mentioned Shakespeare's *King Lear* and can find similarly powerful experiences of "the coming of age," of facing who one really is, or of facing choices we have to make, in Jane Austen's *Emma*, Richard Hughes' *A High Wind in Jamaica*, Mark Twain's *The Adventures of Huckleberry Finn*, and Emily Brontë's *Wuthering Heights*. Many authorities suggest organizing a literature curriculum around the interests of adolescents, but point out that this need not be a limiting factor. Rather, it can be a starting point in developing a program that is a "developmental exploration" leading students to confront more "sophisticated and intellectually challenging questions at each grade level."[1] Selections for such exploration are found both in the classics and in more recent young adult literature.

Frustrated parents and some teachers have often been heard to say that they "give up"—all their daughters appear to be interested in are *boys* and their sons . . . sports and acne. Why should these characteristics be frustrat-

---

[1]Quoted in Probst,   p. 203.

ing? We suspect it is because we are attempting to interest them (the boys and girls, that is) in things that may be better left till later.

Perhaps we should capitalize on these interests as a way of "hooking" adolescents to literature. So what if they don't swoon over Keats' "La Belle Dame Sans Merci"? or a Shakespearean love sonnet? They can, however, explore their passions through books that present adolescent perceptions of the ranges and kinds of love. *Romeo and Juliet* does a pretty good job of exploring the consequences of loving someone of whom parents don't approve. Furthermore, in contrast to the sometimes superficial representation of adolescent "passions" in popular magazines, the play presents its own potential strength, beauty, and steadfastness. Remember Juliet's impassioned dismissal of sweet-nothings when Romeo swears his everlasting love with the romantic moon as his witness?

R: Lady, by yonder blessed moon I swear,
   That tips with silver all these fruit-tree tops—

J: Oh, swear not by the moon, th' inconstant moon,
   that monthly changes in her circled orb,
   Lest that thy love prove likewise variable.

R: What shall I swear by?

J: Do not swear at all. Or, if thou wilt, swear
   by thy gracious self. . .

Romeo and Juliet, Act II, sc. ii

From contemporary young adult literature we can draw a related example from Katherine Paterson's *Jacob Have I Loved*, a brilliant exploration of the struggle of a twin to discover herself while in the shadow of her more sparkling, musically gifted sister.

. . . There was no place to run to, no tip of the marsh where I could sit alone on a stump of driftwood and watch the water. I wanted to cry and scream and throw things. Instead, under almost perfect control, I got a broom and began savagely to attack the sand that was stuck like cement in the corner of the living room.

Katherine Paterson, *Jacob Have I Loved*

The intensity of love/hate, guilt/remorse pulls us back to adolescence and its incredible swings of mood, unreasonableness, black holes, and soaring wonder in a very compelling way. We adults find it quite simple to forget the intensity of these feelings, having long ago worked reason into the matrix of our emotions.

However, just because we survived those topsy-turvy years without the aid of literature that presented us with realistic images of ourselves and our experiences (i.e., adolescent fiction) is not an argument for continuing to expect current students to do the same. Today's high school population is not identical to that of the 1970s and 1980s. Everywhere we read of high school students who do not "buy" the authority of schooling today. If nothing else, television and suggestions of alternatives to the status quo have eroded much of our traditional authority. In many classrooms we can see the impact of irrelevant curricula and teaching styles—students slouching over desks, paying the minimum amount of attention to what is happening in order to get by and, interestingly enough, still able to get by. At the same time, to exclude the classics on the grounds of irrelevance denies adolescents the opportunity to explore themselves and their concerns from other perspectives. Our dress, manners, and even language may change but the issues of life that face all of us (e.g., choices, ethics/morality, love, jealousy, what to do with one's life) *are* timeless: To assume that we can hook every student would be foolish. But to assume that our high school students are as naive as we think they are is also foolish.

> Dear Chrissy. . . .
>
> As soon as I get home I'm planning on having a party. I may or may not invite boys. I may or may not invite Alice Ingram, since I haven't heard from her once. Have you grown any this year? I've hardly grown at all. No up and not out, either. But I have learned a lot. Do you know the difference between helium and hydrogen? Do you know how babies get made? Have you kissed any boys? I have. I will tell you about that too. It's more interesting than the difference between helium and hydrogen.
>
> Judy Blume, *Starring Sally J. Freedman as Herself*

Intellectual/Cognitive Development

Various people have commented on the depth of intellectual development exhibited by adolescents. Linguistically, this is often manifested in their attraction to metaphor, to irony and, hence, levels of meaning. In humor, we see it in their love for punning, double entendres, nonsequiturs, parodies, and caricature.

According to developmental psychologists (Piagetian), adolescents are capable of thinking about fanciful problems not based in reality; they can apply logical rules that apply to ideas that violate reality; think in increasingly flexible and abstract ways; solve problems through logical processes having considered all possibilities; and are capable of making hypothetical judgments.

Related to these intellectual developments, social psychologists have found that adolescents are capable of notions of relativity when applied to behaviors that may, therefore, vary depending on internal states, external situations, or other transitory factors. Adolescents are capable of seeing networks or systems of perspectives (e.g., society's perspectives versus their own alternative points of view relating to group identity), and they are capable of being aware of the full complexity of human thoughts, feelings, and intentions.

More recently, we have begun to realize that many of these capabilities are also related to intellectual experiences that adolescents have in their own lives both in and out of school. Potentially, we may find that the more literate adolescent will exhibit many more of these capabilities—an argument, perhaps, for promoting extensive reading for this and previous age groups.

How might we capitalize on these potentials in the literature classroom? As we see with the tenth-grade essay on *Animal Farm* (Chapter 9), asking students to consider a hypothetical argument such as whether or not the novel is simply an animal story written for children or a symbolic representation of power is not beyond their capabilities. However, beginning with the abstract is possibly where we develop the switch-off attitude we have also observed in high school classrooms.

Although the stated preoccupations of adolescents are usually related to their own emerging adulthood, their need for social and, particularly, peer acceptance, their increased sense of their own inadequacies (figure, hair color, clothes, gamesmanship, height and so on), we don't believe that we must focus exclusively on these preoccupations in order to hook them to literature.

According to library surveys of the most popular types of fiction drawn from adolescent fiction shelves, mystery, suspense, fantasy (particularly science fiction and fantasy) are also popular among this age group. A study of the topics and issues that most concern high school students showed that nuclear holocaust and the declining environment were the two greatest concerns. Post-holocaust dystopias from H.G. Wells to Ursula LeGuin are popular choices from the shelves of public libraries. Not every book has to deal with "growing up," "coming of age," "the agony of young love," etc. Among the classics, both Tolkien and Poe are popular. Many students like e. e. cummings, George Bernard Shaw, the Brontës. Furthermore, many of the classics with adult heroes and heroines deal with themes that will intrigue adolescents if only because these characters face situations that adolescents know are related to adulthood. Our point here is that adolescents need not be restricted to books that deal only with the heavier issues of life, often focused on in contemporary realistic fiction:

"Mama, it is wrong of me I know, but I confess that I like fairy tales."

"And why?"

"Because I like anything that is marvelous, extraordinary . . . metamorphoses, crystal palaces, gold and silver . . . all that enchants me."

Paul Hazard, *Books, Children and Men*

Discussing Literature Knowing Who Adolescents Are

Let's draw the various threads of the chapter together so that we might explore literature with the adolescents, knowing whom we are dealing with. The primary fact is that they know more than we have believed them to know and allowed them to reveal in the traditionally run literature classroom where we emphasize "the theme," "the plot," "the meaning," and so on. We thought we'd start with the first two-thirds of Pooh's dream song in response to hearing that his animal friends were going to give him a party, but his fear is that no one knows what he did to deserve it:

> 3 Cheers for Pooh!
> (For Who?)
> For Pooh—
> (Why, what did he do?)
> I thought you knew;
> He saved his friend from a wetting!
> 3 Cheers for Bear!
> (For Bear—)
> He couldn't swim,
> But he rescued him!
> (He rescued who?)
> Oh listen, do!
> I am talking of Pooh—
> (Of who?)
> Of Pooh!
> (I'm sorry I keep forgetting).
> We'll, Pooh was a Bear of Enormous Brain
> (Just say it again!)
> Of enormous brain—
> (Of enormous what?)
> Well, he ate a lot,
> And I don't know if he could swim or not,
> But he managed to float
> On a sort of boat
> (On a sort of what?)
> Well, a sort of pot—
> So now let's give him three hearty cheers
> (So now let's give him three hearty whiches?)
> And hope he'll be with us for years and years,
> And grow in health and wisdom and riches!
>
> A. A. Milne, *Winnie-the-Pooh*

We too can celebrate the qualities of adolescents or we can make fun of them and see them as irritating things we have to bypass in order to get on with the task we have set for them. We may not want to go as far as Moffett's student-centered curriculum but we can have a student-sensitive classroom. Such a classroom would give these students the opportunity to voice what they know and to permit them to open our own eyes to new perspectives on what we read together. Such a classroom would not require every student to share the same understanding or perspective of the same literary work. Let's have a look at some of the comments adolescents have made about literature they have read.

"I like poetry like this; it's sensitive."

"I thought [of *Brave New World*] that it was pretty fascinating that in 1940 he's seen all those trends in our societies."

"If this guy had really loved youth . . . he wouldn't have turned the boy in but also you could see it like he loved him enough to turn him back to his father . . . but it seemed . . . he would have more taken the side of the boy."

"You could take it literally . . . or it could have sort of more deep meaning like . . . you can't trust adults."

"It's weird in the end because you can't really say that he's a traitor because he says . . . 'you ought to make him happy.' "

"They're searching for themselves . . . and eventually, that finally happens . . . they're really beautiful books."

"The Indian boy was kind of a small and skinny thing . . . he is a stubborn boy and is also curious and thinks about things a lot . . . . And he just didn't like grown-ups because he had to go to school and didn't have much freedom."

"It tells a story about people's outlook on life. The guy that wrote it must have been a real philosopher."

We strongly argue in Chapter 5 and elsewhere in this book for a great deal of small-group and large-group discussion of literature. However, given that we have also said adolescents are very peer oriented and dislike, more than other age groups, to stand out alone, we suggest that the more idiosyncratic response, that which reflects the reader's own experiences most closely, is more likely to occur when we allow for open-response situations. Outside the classroom, we've seen that, given the opportunity, adolescents can have a great deal to say about literature, without needing "guidance" or prompting. So what's good about letting them tread unknown paths at least some of the time?

In answer to this question, we need to go back to what we've argued elsewhere about becoming readers. Developing expertise as a reader is obviously a cumulative experience. Even very competent and experienced readers may flounder when first encountering a text that presents information in an unfamiliar form and language. The information itself may be very unfamiliar, in which case our early attempts at discerning meaning in the text are, at best, exploratory ones. But that solo exploration is also a part of becoming a competent reader.

We have heard teachers say that when they ask students "what the story means" (if very unfamiliar) and don't get responses, they feel obliged to fill in and give them the answers. Maybe they are asking the wrong question. Try asking what the words say. Similarly, having large- or small-group discussions does not ensure that all readers in the group will have negotiated the meaning of the text for themselves. Yet, however "off the wall" or "wide of the mark" an individual interpretation may be, we believe it is necessary to allow students to experience some solo interpretive activity at some point as a means of developing the confidence required to offer a perspective at some other time (e.g., sitting for the ACT or SAT).

More importantly, we also believe that confidence in one's own negotiation of meaning in a text is a precursor to the development of individual appreciation of literature. If we are continually dependent on others for defining meaning in text we will not experience the levels of enjoyment and aesthetic appreciation that are possible when we have a well-developed sense of content and context ourselves.

The diversity in response, rather than being something to frown upon or sigh over, may, in fact, represent just the elusive individualized engagement with text that we, paradoxically, also hope for, as these responses to Eudora Welty's story "A Worn Path" suggest:

SM: I think this story had a lot to do with determination; the way that the old lady kept going on her long journey, even though she sometimes forgot why she was traveling.

TE: Themes in "A Worn Path" is that of age. Age is very important. The fact that the story is called that suggests a used, old, path, worn out with time. The woman using the path is very old, and can't even remember why she is going to where she is going.

WC: "A Worn Path" is about a conflict between old and young in post-Reformation Mississippi. The old woman is caught between the young and old in "A Worn Path."

DT: There are several themes in "A Worn Path." The main theme is the theme of love. . . . The old woman's love for her grandson was very great. She went to much trouble to please him. This is why I think that the theme is love.

B: Phoenix Jackson represents people who live with self-doubt and who don't believe in themselves.

GD: Phoenix Jackson is a symbol of determination in people no matter what happens or how old and tired they are.

JD: I think this story has a theme of appearance compared to reality. Phoenix acts like a batty old lady, and it seems strange for her to make such a long trip, but she has a good reason. She looks too old to go that far, but she's done it regularly for three years. You can't take this old lady at face value.

CHAPTER 3

Being a Chapter That Deals in Literary Theory and Its Relation to the Curriculum

Before we go into any detail about the response-centered literature curriculum we recommend, we think it might be useful to discuss some of the major issues and controversies surrounding the teaching of literature at the end of the twentieth century. These include the issue of culture and cultural literacy, the issue of current curricular theories and their definitions of text and reader and writer, and the issue of what literature and literature study is.

The content of literature instruction is usually limited to five basic groups of items: literary works, background information, literary terminology and theory, cultural information, and the responses of the students themselves. In terms of what students are to do with all this content, the foci of the curriculum range from recognition and recall through interpretation and evaluation to the categories of preference and value. We will set up our particular model later in the chapter.

The shifts of emphasis within these boundaries depend upon the purposes of the curriculum-makers and their particular philosophic penchants, which are influenced by nationalism, scientism, pragmatism, and moralism among other ideological pressures. Teachers have to negotiate their own objectives with those of principals, curriculum specialists, school boards, state mandates, parents, testing companies, and the students.

Through all these shifts of perspective, literature as a subject is viewed through one of three main sets of lenses. One set sees it primarily as a body of knowledge to be acquired; the second set sees it as the vehicle for the training of the critical skills of analysis and interpretation; the third set sees it as the vehicle for social and moral development. Many curriculum-makers have sought to combine these three approaches in various ways, and many actual curricula represent pragmatic choices to reconcile the different objectives. The knowledge and values approaches both suggest that a curriculum planner must attend to the selection of texts, either focusing on the "approved" author or on the supposed moral and social content of the text. Both approaches also suggest that the major behaviors are those of knowledge and preference, rather than analysis and interpretation. Both also can be used by political conservatives or liberals, as witness the debate on cultural literacy, which we'll take up first. The ideas of the critical skills approach can be seen in the "new critical," "deconstructive," "Marxist," or "reader-response" approaches to literature. Some people also want the literature curriculum to serve something called "generic critical thinking skills." They argue that it doesn't matter what text the students are reading as long as they learn a procedure. We think that literature texts do matter.

What About This Cultural Literacy Business?

Although cultural literacy has come into the news recently the idea is far from new. The notion of a "culture" goes back at least as far as the eighteenth century. As Edward Said notes, culture is "all that which an individual possesses and which possesses an individual." As he writes in *The World, the Text and the Critic*:

> . . . culture is used to designate not merely something to which one belongs but something that one possesses, and along with that proprietary process, culture also designates a boundary by which the concept of what is extrinsic or intrinsic to the culture comes into forceful play. (Edward Said, pp. 8–9)

Anthropologists tend to see culture somewhat differently from literary people, but this root definition of possession and being possessed applies both to family groups and to groups that people join when they leave the family—a community, a school, a profession or trade, a regional or national group. Current "American" culture is a culture of affiliation, whether it be the culture of Hawthorne and Harriet Beecher Stowe, the culture of black studies, the culture of feminism, or the culture of punk.

Any culture usually tries to isolate its members from other cultures, and any culture is elitist and exclusionary by definition. People who have a culture see others as outsiders or beneath them. We are all snobs with respect to one "them" or another. Very few people transcend cultures or are full members of more than one culture. Many of us do switch from one subculture to another as we go through life. We may be reader-response researchers in the United States, who have our body of shared knowledge, our set of allegiances to I.A. Richards, Louise Rosenblatt, and James Squire, and our tendency to exclude those who, even though very well educated in other respects, fail to share our knowledge and beliefs. Some of us may also be members of such other subcultures as that of mycologists, joggers, film freaks, sailors, Poles, English teachers, as well as members of the broader culture of literate Americans.

Joining the Canon Club

To be a member of a culture, one must possess a fair amount of knowledge, some of it tacit, concerning the culture: its rules, its rituals, its little customs, its heroes, gods, and demigods. This knowledge lies at the heart of cultural literacy, and the knowledge is brought into play when people read and respond to a piece of literature that comes from the same culture. It is such knowledge, in fact, that enables them to read that literature. By knowledge, one must include semantic knowledge, knowledge of text structures and models, and pragmatic knowledge or knowledge as to how to act before, during, and after reading a particular text in a given situation. It is these kinds of knowledge that are brought into play when we read and write as social beings. The lack of such knowledge keeps us outside, as witnessed by the problems of visitors to our culture who often suffer trifling embarrassments or serious misunderstandings.

How the Curriculum Helps

Given the idea of culture, one function of a literature curriculum in a school-language program is to bring students into a broader culture than that of their home. We want them to read and come to know stories, poems, plays, and essays that they will have in common with other people. The questions are which ones? and who decides?

A second function is to promote loyalty, acceptance, and valuing of those works and literature generally. We'd like culturally literate Americans to praise Mark Twain as a great writer and be offended when someone calls for the banning of *Huckleberry Finn*.

A third function of literature education is the development of individuality. Once a student has learned to share the culture and developed a loyalty to it, then a student should strike out to read new things, and write them too.

Some of the cultural literacy advocates, however, are only interested in the first two functions. They want to restrict literacy to a particular culture, such as the "Great Tradition" or "the humanities" or "the American classics." They refer to a definite body of knowledge and suggest that specific titles are necessary. It is this common knowledge that enables readers to read certain kinds of texts—notably texts that are shared by a group that one might define as "highly literate Americans." These would be people, for example, who can read *The New York Times* with understanding and can also read journals and books such as *The Atlantic Monthly* or Katherine Paterson's *Jacob Have I Loved.*

One argument for this sort of cultural literacy was that such literacy brought together a disparate immigrant population and helped the melting pot do its job. Such proposals bore with them the arguments of people like Matthew Arnold, Ralph Waldo Emerson, and T.S. Eliot, not to mention the major universities and educational reformers, that a common culture or the Judeo-Christian American Heritage forged society into unity through affiliation. Even if only a small elite were so educated, the idea was that there would be a filtering to the masses.

It does so not without cost.

> When our students are taught such things as "the humanities" they are almost always taught that these classic texts embody, express, represent what is best in our, that is, the only, tradition. Moreover, they are taught that such fields as the humanities and such subfields as "literature" exist in a relatively neutral political element, that they are to be appreciated and venerated, that they define the limits of what is acceptable, appropriate, and legitimate as far as culture is concerned. (Said, p. 21)

The cultural literacy issue has raised a number of political questions— particularly, who is to select the unifying texts? A second question is how in the political history of our educational system did the idea of the cultural heritage come to disappear and why should the lack of a cultural center now become a political issue.

The Attack on the Canon Club

About fifteen years ago a number of groups began to coalesce to push literature and the notion of cultural literacy out of the forefront of the English curriculum. The first group advocated making the secondary school comprehensive; the second group was made up of the linguists, the third of so-called functionalists, and the fourth were the literature teachers themselves. Their arguments against a single canon and against a focus on literature can be enumerated as follows:

1. We have a comprehensive secondary school system even though some individual schools are specialized, and more diverse groups are .

now passing through it. We must attend to the cultural needs of those groups. The canon does not address these minority groups and it certainly does not address the concerns of women. In addition, the world is multicultural and students need to learn a smattering about all cultures. Perhaps it is unnecessary to learn about any.

2. English education should be dominated by language study and the appropriate teaching of the uses of language, whether one adopts a skills approach or whether one adopts an approach that looks at the personal growth of the individual student. There is no time for literature as such.

3. English education should meet the functional needs of the students and the workplace. There is little room in life for the cultural heritage.

4. Many of the "classics" are simply too difficult for the new students and beyond their range of experience. They were appropriate for people of greater and broader and different experiences of life—the elite. Rather than bowdlerize them or present them in film, we should turn to the kinds of works that students can read, particularly adolescent and popular fiction.

Those who push for cultural literacy using the argument of the unification of a diverse nation through cultural literacy have not addressed these arguments. The argument is not *whether* cultural literacy, for all literature curricula imply a body of works that constitute a canon and thus serve to acculturate youth, as do television and other nonschool phenomena; rather, the argument is *what* should serve to define the culture or cultures of our society.

Our response to the four arguments is to wholeheartedly accept the first one and reject the other three. Language and literacy do not make any sense without literature, because it is literature that binds us as a nation, a nation made up of interesting and quirky subgroups. Literature is functional in our lives, and it supports and sustains us as individuals and groups. Young people have a remarkably broad range of experience. People do other things besides work, and even in their work there is a place for the comfort and relief as well as the intellectual stimulation of reading and feeling satisfied by the experience of a text. As to the fourth charge, we haven't yet met a work of literature that is too difficult for any group of students given a good teacher; the only difficult works are those the culture boys set up on the pedestal and say are too hard for the masses, thereby intimidating students.

So we are for cultural literacy. We want to broaden the definition and include both Shakespeare and Achebe; Austen and Baraka, Homer and Plath; Thomas Wolfe and Tom Wolfe. Some we think are more central than others, and we want both the center and the fringes. Students should join the Canon Club but be free to join others too.

Now That We Aren't Sure About Culture, What About Literature?

Let's try some definitions. Texts are artifacts produced by a type of person that one calls writer or author. Texts possess in common the broad features of having a content (that subject matter or referential world with which they deal), a structure, and a set of distinctive linguistic features often referred to as style and tone. These divisions are ones that readers and writers often make even though the readers and writers realize that the sum of the text is greater than its parts, and that the text may be perceived as an organic whole.

A Functional Definition of Literature

Writers may have in mind a variety of functions for the text they are writing when they write. Readers may also see a given text as having one of a number of functions as they read it: to say something about language itself, to say something about the writer, to say something about the reader, to say something about the world outside the text, to keep open the channel of communication, or to invite everyone to participate in the text itself (this last is called the *poetic function* by many). No writer or reader perceives any one text as being a pure representative of a single function. The functions mix and the labels are only partial descriptors. Nonetheless, they may prove useful.

Different communities of readers tend to focus on one or more of these functions as they deal with a text or a body of texts. These communities are the same as classrooms or schools but they may also be religious, business, social, or ethnic groups. One of these groups may say that a certain set of texts are poetic, that they are literature. Literature doesn't exist as a separate category of text that can be defined in terms of certain internal characteristics. Rather, literary texts tend to be those that communities of readers perceive as such, which is to say that they are texts that a significant number of readers read for the experience of reading the text rather than to get information or draw moral guidance from. They will say that they read these texts aesthetically and claim others should so read them.

Literature From a Reader's Perspective

Literature is often defined as the verbal expression of the human imagination, a definition broad enough to encompass a vast array of genres and forms of discourse. Recent literary theory has come to view literature less in terms of the writer and more in terms of the reader, for it appears to be the reader, particularly the informed and trained reader, who defines a text as literary. Such a definition allows for all sorts of works, which once had been excluded or were marginal (essays, letters, biographies, and the like), to be part of the literary canon. There is some sense in which the traditional literary genres of drama, poetry, and fiction have a more dominant role in most critics' thinking and thus a more prominent place in the curriculum than the other sorts of works. It is clear, however, that any definition must be such as to allow for new genres and new media.

Such a definition is closely related to the theoretical base that follows from the strand of thinking that says the reader helps form the meaning of the text. This position is best summarized by Louise Rosenblatt in *The Reader, the Text, the Poem* (1978), who says that literary texts are grounded in the real world of writers who may intend them to be seen poetically or not. Once written, texts become alive only when they are read, and they become "literary" when a sufficient body of readers (a community) chooses to read them as aesthetic objects rather than as documents. These readers bring a great deal of background knowledge concerning the substance, structure, and style of the texts in order to ascertain the meaning and significance of the text. The meaning is that which can be verified by other readers of the text and by recourse to the historical grounding of the text, if such is available. The significance is personal or perhaps communal.

So What Makes Up Literature?

This theoretical position argues that any text has the potential of being literary, should a significant group of knowledgeable and experienced readers determine the value of reading the text as an aesthetic object. In this way such works as the speeches of Abraham Lincoln and Martin Luther King, Jr., the letters of John Keats and Hector Crèvecoeur, and the *Diary of Anne Frank* become literary objects and part of the canon. Readers have read them in the light of a common experience of literary texts and have derived principles of "literariness," which allows them to accept these works. In part, their criteria are formal and structural; in part, they arise from consideration of the breadth of vision of the writer.

In a society such as that of the United States, there may exist a set of texts that the community refers to as "literature," which is to say that these texts are to be viewed functionally as being predominantly poetic and therefore to be read aesthetically. At the same time other communities within the society may read those texts as informing or persuading (or perhaps like a greeting card—who ever really listens to the sense of "The Night Before Christmas"?). These different communities may also focus their attention primarily on the content, structure, or style and tone depending on their view of the function of the text within the community.

As a result of this communal process, a network of texts grows over time and forms part of the background that weaves a group into a community. From this communal nature of texts comes one of the well-known features of literature—its tendency to feed upon itself as well as upon folklore, myth, and historical events. Many literary works are clearly situated in a web of culture, just as many others are situated in a specific time and place (e.g., Jonathan Swift's works, which are clearly situated in eighteenth-century England). We may argue that when a writer selects a given word, he or she is doing so with a penumbra of associations and references that are peculiarly the writer's and the writer's culture, and have reference to the writer's reading as well as his or her conversations and other linguistic experiences. Literature uses allusion, and many writers presume background knowledge on the part of the reader even though the allusions have been transmuted into a new artifact. Nonliterary texts also presume much the same knowledge. But there is the difference that literary texts form part of a large textual world that is interdependent and which forms that thing called literature. So the literary community determines. From this grouping of texts comes one part of the literature curriculum—but only a part. We're back at a canon again.

A group of texts, then, has been set aside by communities as forming a part of the communal experience. These communities have selected them to be read aesthetically. By virtue of that fact, the texts have developed a set of associations with each other. Subsequent writers acculturated into this "tradition" have produced texts that are highly allusive to this communal set of literature. We might add that what has happened in the literary world has also happened in certain transnational disciplines such as psychology and economics. Certain texts have emerged as a core upon which other texts have built. The core in both cases is added to, challenged, and at times drops certain writers and texts as it adds others. It is a fluid corpus, not a fixed canon; the organic metaphor is quite appropriate.

Literature as Content

This brings us back to the "content" of literature curricula, which consist primarily of a group of literary texts, perhaps specified by genre, date, theme, author, and other classifications. The particular texts are set in part by experts, in part by those who sell books, and in part by teachers and curriculum planners. There are other broad areas of literature content too: historical and background information concerning authors, texts, and the times in which they were written or that form their subject matter; information concerning critical terminology, critical strategies, and literary theory; information of a broad cultural nature such as that emerging from folklore and mythology, which forms a necessary starting point for the reading of many literary texts.

To these we add another dimension, the crucial element in the curriculum: the responses of the students themselves. As we suggested in the opening chapter, the important aspect of literature in our view is that it is read, and that it is not the text out there apart from the reader that is important but the text as it is read and made into a poem or a play or a novel and shared with the group.

OK, So What About All This Deconstruction and Semiotics and Reader-Response Stuff?

The recent critical debates raise issues that should have affected the curriculum in literature—but they did not as far as we can tell. And that is the reason behind this book. The main point of most of recent literary theory can be stated thus: Texts are written by authors, deal with something called "the world," and are read by readers. It used to be that we looked at literature primarily as reflecting the world. Then we thought of texts as the outpourings of their authors. Then we thought of them as isolated specimens to be examined. Now we think of them as things read by people. Today, texts are seen as situated in an intertextual world, and they have an indeterminancy of meaning dependent upon the varying experiences and natures of the readers. Meaning and text themselves are not objective. In fact, there may not be much of an objective world.

I think, therefore there is thinking.

It used to be that we thought of the purposefully ambiguous nature of the text. It was hard to get scholars and teachers to agree on the correct interpretation of *Hamlet* or Robert Frost's "Mending Wall." The problem lay in the text and the author's deliberate plot to confuse us. It is still hard to get them to agree. The problem lies in the readers.   *Cite text* —

As we said, the readers will disagree on the text's function and therefore its "meaning." It used to be that the text was seen as the norm by which a reading and a response could be judged. Now it is no longer the norm—even theoretically. The norms—if there are any—lie in the community of readers—even the two people who talk about a book over coffee. Some argue that the largest community we can find is a classroom. Others would say that there are larger communities, such as those dominated by examination systems or textbook publishers.

This change in the critical view shifts the focus to the readers—that is to say, the students in our schools. It is no longer sufficient to talk about texts or critical terminology or history. We must talk about readers. We must talk and plan the curriculum, taking into account the ways by which the readers make the texts come alive. That means focusing on what they say and do. Literature comes out of the textbooks and into the minds and hearts, and particularly the mouths and pens of our students. That is what the critical shift has done to the curriculum—or what it should do. The current textbook series pay lip service to this approach to literature teaching. Unfortunately, they still have the teachers' guides with all the "right" answers.

Theorists argue that literature education is a combination of reading and some form of articulation of a reasoned response to what is read, at times through dramatic interpretation, at times through discussion, at times through writing. The poem does not exist unless the reader makes some overt commitment to it.

Research shows that readers within a culture tend to have similar impressions of the poems, stories, and plays that they read. Where they differ is in their power of expression concerning what they have read. The "better" or more "experienced" reader is the one who can set forth a more reasoned and detailed account of the poem he or she has created in his or her head. It is the expression and the statements about the poem that causes the disagreement among critics, not the experience of reading the text.

OK. You've Talked About the Canon and About Literary Theory, But How Does This Get Put Together into the Curriculum? Are You Ready for the Scheme?

Let us try to see where all this talk about the canon and knowledge and literature and language arts and English all fit together.

School literature is usually seen as one of the language arts, which have often been defined in terms of reading, writing, speaking, and listening. Because literature involves texts that people read or write, and because when students read literature they often write about what they have read, literature is often seen as simply a subset of reading and writing, with an occasional nod to speaking and listening.

But we're uneasy with this definition. We become more uneasy when students look at the world of tests and see that literature is simply a vehicle for reading comprehension tests or for measures of writing skill or proficiency. There's something more. To define the literature curriculum as simply a subset of reading and writing neglects a number of the acts that go on within the activity of literature education.

Literature as a school subject has its own body of knowledge. This is all that content that we said people often bring to their reading of a new text.

We also see literature as something that is read differently. This kind of reading we call "aesthetic" and oppose it to the reading that you do with informational texts. Thus, a part of literature education is the development of what one might call preferences, which is to say habits of mind in reading and writing. You have to learn to read aesthetically and to switch lenses when you move from social studies to poetry.

In addition, literature education is supposed to develop something called "taste" or the love of "good literature," so that literature education goes beyond reading and writing in the inculcation of specific sets of preferences and habits of reading and writing about that particular body of texts called literature.

We may then conclude that the domain of school literature can be divided into three interrelated aspects: knowledge, practice, and choice. The interrelationships are complex in that one uses knowledge in the various acts that constitute the practice and the preferences, and that the practices and preferences can have their influence on knowledge. At the same time one can separate them for the purposes of curriculum planning and, as we shall see, testing. We may schematize the three subdomains as follows:

SCHOOL LITERATURE

Knowledge		Practice		Preferences	
Textual	*Extratextual*	*Responding*	*Articulating*	*Aesthetic*	*Habits*
Specific text	History	Decoding	Re-creating	Evaluating	Reading
Cultural allusion	Author	Envisioning	Criticizing single works	Selecting	Criticizing
	Genres	Analyzing		Valuing	
	Styles	Personalizing	Generalizing across works		
	Responses				
	Critical works and terms	Interpreting			

We have a bit of shorthand here. The cultural knowledge can be contained in texts like myths and folktales or it can exist outside of texts. We have used the term *responding* to cover reading, watching, listening. We see it includes decoding or making out the plain sense of the text or film; envisioning, or coming to some whole impression and re-creation of what is read; and the more detailed aspects of analyzing, personalizing, and interpreting. Often people envision without analyzing or interpreting.

We have used the term *articulating* to cover a wide variety of ways by which students let people know what their response is. This is the key to the curriculum in many ways. It's not just reading in a closet. It's bringing a vision of what is read out into the open—sharing, baring, stumbling, formulating, changing, reflecting, and, above all, publicizing the response that the curriculum is all about. It is about becoming a part of the community—the community of the classroom and the broader community beyond the classroom.

All of this is done in a particular way that preserves the aesthetic nature of the text and treats the work of literature as literature, not as a treatise on whales.

The curriculum we are setting forth in the next chapter is one that focuses on discourse about the texts. It seeks to help students become more reasoning and reasonable, more articulate about what they have read—to help them share their expressions and to find their place in their community as well as to discover their individuality.

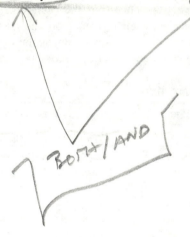

BOTH / AND

CHAPTER 4

Enter (Stage Right) the Response-Centered Curriculum

A response-centered approach to literature will help introduce students to the canon and the community and retain their individuality. It will allow for aesthetic reading. Above all, it will aid students in articulating their responses. It also cures psoriasis and leaves drains shiny bright.

Four Objectives of a Response-Centered Literature Curriculum

1. An individual will feel secure in his response to a poem and not be dependent on someone else's response. An individual will trust himself.
2. An individual will know why she responds the way she does to a poem—what in her causes that response and what in the poem causes that response. She will get to know herself.
3. An individual will respect the responses of others as being as valid for them as his is for him. He will recognize his differences from other people.
4. An individual will recognize that there are common elements in people's responses. She will recognize her similarity with other people.

> The basic process connecting the onlooker with any event, real or fictional, involving living things, is that of imagining. The fundamental fact is that we can imagine ourselves in a situation very different from the one we are in, we can create images of the sensations we should have, we can become aware, in part, of the meanings we should see in it, what our intentions, attitudes, and emotions would be, what satisfactions and frustrations we should experience.
>
> D. W. Harding

"Response-centered program" is a fairly accurate definition of the way we suggest literature should be taught. We are here making a specific application of a general approach to curriculum suggested by many of contemporary curriculum workers and theoreticians.

Of course, you don't teach literature, or English—you teach students. We all know that. People, not things, are the focus of instruction. Recently, too much attention has been paid to things, and people have been forgotten.

Naturally, people learn all by themselves. People have done it for years. They have learned lots of things without teachers, and outside classrooms. One of the best ways people have devised for learning is by doing things and then by figuring out what they have done and why they have done it. If they like what they have done, they try to repeat the operation.

Doing things and looking at yourself while and after you have done them is what this program is about.

That's why this is a response-centered program. It is not focused only on the students. Nor is it focused entirely on the literary works and literature. It's not subject centered or student centered. It deals with what happens when student meets subject. That way, it's student-and-subject centered.

But we like to call it response centered. Because responding—responding creatively—is what people do.

There's a poem, written by somebody, and that somebody has a life and a history and an environment.

There's a reader who is somebody with his world of images, metaphors, symbols; and that somebody has a life and a history and an environment.

One reader reads the poem and something happens:

she understands what the words say to her

she translates the experience she has read about into her own context

she has a feeling about the experience

she has attitudes about the experience and the poem

she reaches conclusions and makes judgments.

Another way of putting it: Another reader takes the words, and the images, and the experiences and ideas of that poem; and he puts them into his own way of seeing things. He reads a poem with the word *snapped*.

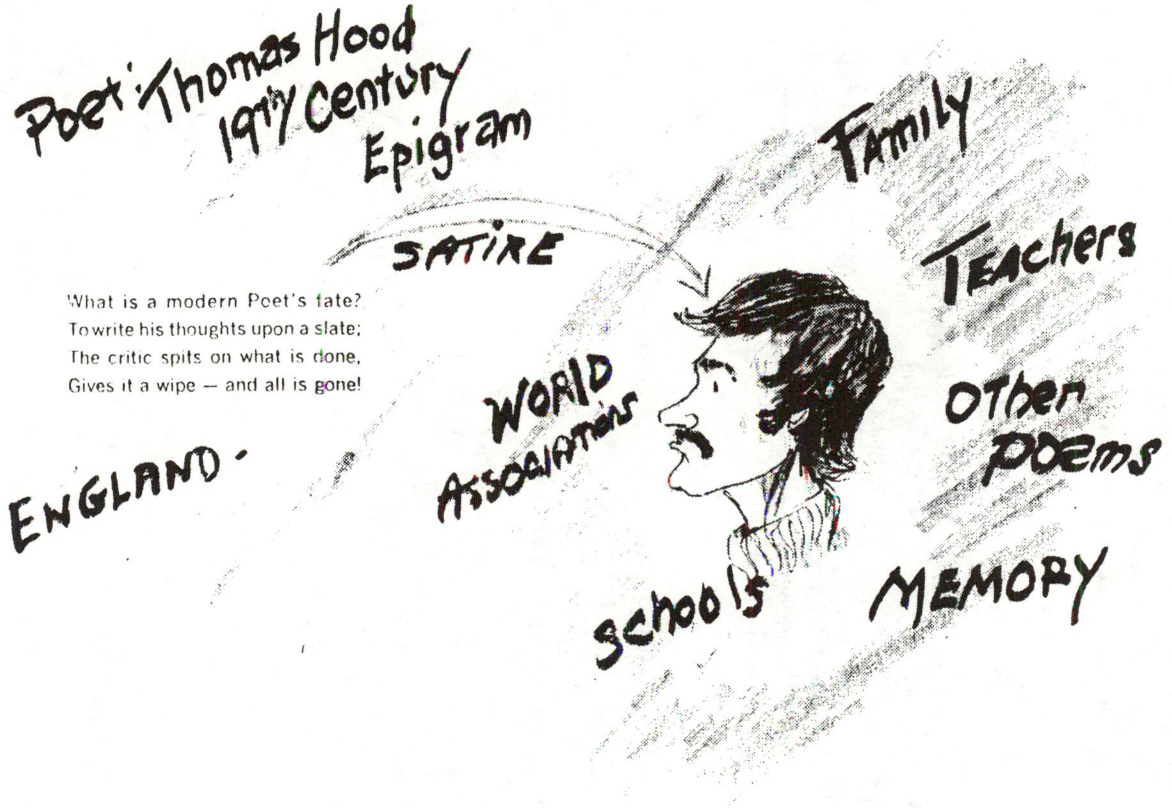

Family

Teachers

Other Poems

Memory

Schools

Associations

World

Satire

Poet: Thomas Hood
19th Century
Epigram

England

What is a modern Poet's fate?
To write his thoughts upon a slate:
The critic spits on what is done,
Gives it a wipe — and all is gone!

Maybe he sees a gingersnap, maybe he sees someone snapping her fingers, maybe it makes him feel funny or sad, maybe he doesn't understand that the word could mean to *talk sharply*.

On the basis of that process, the reader might

                                                draw a picture

groan

                    talk about the poem

                                        role-play a character

                  laugh

write a paragraph

                  make a film

                        try to forget he read the silly thing.

That's his response: part of it's inside him, part of it's expressed. We all do it. We've been doing it for years. Even critics do it. Saying we respond to pieces of literature is like saying we have been talking prose all our lives.

The Particular Response Depends on What Is Being Responded to

THEODORE HELPGOD

Stranger! I died of hydrophobia.
I was bitten by both the upper and the under dog.
While trying to save the under dog.

                                      E. L. Masters

THE SUDDEN CHILLNESS

The piercing chill I feel:
    my dead wife's comb, in our bedroom,
        under my heel. . .

                        Taniguchi Buson

Those two are quite different. The pieces differ.

sounds   words   characters   images   locales   incidents

The ways of gluing the pieces together differ

arrangements   syntax   plot   structure   pattern   tone
mood   voice   total shape

You could even take the same pieces and glue them differently and get a different work.

Stranger, While trying to save the underdog,
I was bitten by both the upper and the under dog.
I died of hydrophobia.

The Particular Response We Make Depends on Who Is Responding

People differ in their experience. Many have never been to the seashore. Many have read lots of comic books. Some have been in wars. Some have lost a father or a mother. Some come from another culture or spoke another language. Their past experiences affect their response.

People differ in their concepts of things. Say "America" to a group of ten people and ask them to say what their concept of it is. You probably will get ten different concepts. But you can find common threads.

People differ in their attitudes toward things. Not everybody hates school or poetry or phys ed.

People differ in their interests. Not everybody watches the same TV game show. Some even turn off the set.

All of these and many other differences affect even the way people perceive things. If you love a boy, you see him in a crowd. You don't "see" the other people. If you read a letter, or a list, you see your name, not all the other names.

If these differences affect the way people see things, they also affect the kinds of reactions they have to things, and the kinds of actions they perform in response to things.

Look again at the poems on page 50. Jot down all the things that come to mind. Get a friend to do the same thing. Are the jottings more alike or are they different?

Then do it again next week. How have your jottings changed?

In a reading that results in a work of art, the reader is concerned with the quality of the experience that he is living through under the stimulus and guidance of the text. No one else can read the poem or the novel or the play for him. To ask someone else to experience a work of art for him would be tantamount to seeking nourishment by asking someone else to eat his dinner for him.

Louise Rosenblatt

If People Are Different and If Stories and Poems and
Plays Are Different, Then We Can Say That Different
People Respond Differently to Different Pieces of Writing
(or Painting, or Whatever). There Are Only Unique
Responses.

Not quite. Remember what we wrote in the last chapter. There are such
things as communities that bring people together and hold them together too.
Studies of response to literature show that at one level readers from the same
society have the same emotional apprehension of a text. Where they differ, as
we said, is in how clearly and forcefully they can articulate their understanding of that apprehension.

People also generally have common meanings for stories and poems and
plays—or at least common boundaries for meanings. There is difference
within a common framework—diversity within unity.

That's one philosophical principle of this curriculum: to allow for and
foster both individuality and commonality. It's nice to be yourself and part of
a group. You can share without giving up your total independence. Sharing is
important, so is the group.

The literature curriculum seeks to change people. It does not want them
to become one of the herd or total individuals. Both instincts must be
respected. It seeks to challenge them to accept both their commonality and
their individuality.

It also seeks to get them to be careful explorers of themselves and their
readings and the text.

Although works are unique and people are unique and responses are
unique, there are points where responses touch and overlap. The following
are three points of agreement:

> If everybody in a group is responding to the same poem, the common
> point is the poem.
>
> If a person is responding to a poem, a play, and a novel, the common
> point is the person.
>
> If a group of people are discussing novels they have read, the common
> points are the language they use and the community they enter.

The Sea
Poor boy. He had very big ears, and when he would turn his back to the
window they would become scarlet. Poor boy. He was bent over, yellow.
The man who cured came by behind his glasses. "The sea," he said, "the
sea, the sea." Everyone began to pack suitcases and speak of the sea. They
were in a great hurry.

The boy figured that the sea was like being inside a tremendous seashell full of echoes and chants and voices that would call from afar with a long echo. He thought that the sea was tall and green, but when he arrived at the sea, he stood still. His skin, how strange it was there. "Mother," he said because he felt ashamed, "I want to see how high the sea will come on me." He who thought that the sea was tall and green, saw it white like the head of a beer—tickling him, cold on the tips of his toes.

"I am going to see how far the sea will come on me." And he walked, he walked, he walked and the sea, what a strange thing!—grew and became blue, violet. It came up to his knees. Then to his waist, to his chest, to his lips, to his eyes. Then into his ears there came a long echo and the voices that call from afar. And in his eyes all the color. Ah, yes, at last the sea was true. It was one great, immense seashell. The sea truly was tall and green.

But those on the shore didn't understand anything about anything. Above they began to cry and scream and were saying "What a pity, Lord, what a great pity."

Anna Maria Matute

To take the first common point first: A story like the preceding one has a set number of words and a set order of words.

Those words have a limited, although not strictly limited, range of meanings. "Poor" can mean *unfortunate* in not being rich, in not being healthy, in not being happy, in not being lucky, and so forth. . . .

Odds are that it does not mean *happy*.

"The man who cured came by behind his glasses" can hardly be reconstructed as "The glasses who cured came by behind the man" unless you wanted to change what had been written.

A story like the one you've just read has a set order of incidents. The boy goes to the sea after he is at home, not before.

The story also contains only the incidents and people it contains. For the purposes of this story, the boy might as well have no grandfather and no sister. He might or might not have been locked in his room for three weeks prior to the opening of the story. It has a set number of people speaking: a narrator, a boy, a man, some other people. At times it is hard to tell whether the boy or the narrator is speaking, but at those times the choice is limited to those two.

These are some of the limits set by the text.

Here are some limits *not* set by the text:

Whether the boy is sick with tuberculosis

Whether the boy is young or old

Whether the boy wants to die

Whether the man who cured is a doctor or a minister

Whether the narrator likes the boy or not
Whether the narrator approves of the boy
Whether the boy knows that he is going to die
Whether the parents love the boy
Whether he loves his parents
Whether the colors have any significance
Whether the boy is imaginative
Whether the people on the shore are unimaginative or stupid
Whether the narrator agrees with the people on the shore
Whether those on the shore are spiritually dead
Whether those on the shore represent some abstract force or idea
Whether the author admires the boy for what he did
Whether the author agrees with the narrator
Whether the author thinks those on the shore are ignorant
Whether the boy is triumphant, sad, or ironic, or all three
Whether there is a lesson to be learned from the story
Whether the story is well constructed
Whether the story is moving
Whether the story is meaningful to the twentieth-century reader
Whether the story is a classic
Whether the author subscribes to a philosophical position
Whether the whole story takes place in the boy's mind
Whether the author is a great writer
Whether the author is a woman
Whether the author and the story are. . .

To take the second common point: Some of the ways by which an individual's responses to several works may have something in common include the words and word structures she knows; the experiences she has had; the prejudices she has acquired; her ability to tell about the connotation and implication of certain words; whether she can visualize images, or whether her imagination is more auditory or kinetic; her openness to new experiences; the preconceptions she has formed.

To take the third common point: Most people have some things in common.

most people have roughly the same meaning of some words in their heads;
most people have comparable experiences of some things;

most people have similar judgments of human behavior: they know whom to trust, what motivates people to do what they do;

most people have comparable emotional reactions to such things as colors, sound patterns, actions of certain people;

most people make similar judgments about some things, like what they saw if they were watching a television show—they saw a person riding a horse, not a series of light and dark dots.

Most people can agree that it is possible for different people to make different judgments about some things—whether it was a goodie or a baddie riding that horse—and nobody being absolutely sure.

So. . .

the text limits our response

the limits of human nature limit our response

our ability to communicate limits our response

our common humanity limits our response

The major difference between people in the same community when they read and respond to and talk about or write about a piece of literature is not in the reading or response, but in the talk. Research has shown that a person could make over one hundred different kinds of individual statements about a text such as to talk about the language or rhythm or plot or character or setting or interpretation or genre or theme or moral or quality of style or historical period or personal reaction or estimate of worthiness or, or, or. . . .

If you combined five of these individual statements, the resultant option would be one of 500,000,000,000 possible five-sentence paragraphs. Maybe some of them would make sense. It's the combinations of statements that make up the thousands of articles on a single play of Shakespeare; not thousands of different understandings of the play.

If you have taught "The Sea" and ask each student to write an analysis of the boy's motivation or of the meaning of the colors in the story you will get thirty different papers. You would probably find that many of the differences are in the phrasing and organization of the papers.

Yet even the phrasing and organization will have common elements, because the students have learned something of the conventions of writing about stories and they know what sort of writing you expect and reward. They have become part of the community you have established.

Given the diversity and connectedness of people's responses to what they read or see, the educational goal becomes one of helping the students recognize both that diversity and that connectedness.

Enter: The Response-Centered Curriculum

It recognizes people's diversity, and it encourages that diversity.

It recognizes the connections between people and encourages people to make them manifest in sharing their responses with a group.

It recognizes that response is joyous.

Its procedure is simple:

How does it go about it? Through a simple combination:

Take 1 class of mixed students;

Add 1 literary text and

1 teacher—that's the secret ingredient because here is what the teacher does:

There is a great deal for the teacher to do:

The teacher directs the students to themselves and the words of the text.

The teacher provides the students with as many different works as possible.

The teacher encourages all students to respond as fully as they are able.

The teacher challenges the students to understand why they respond as they do.

The teacher encourages the students to respond to as many works as possible.

The teacher provides the students with language to help articulate their responses.

The teacher encourages each student to tolerate responses that differ from the teacher's.

The teacher encourages students to explore their areas of agreement and disagreement.

In the response-centered curriculum, the teacher encourages students to express whatever their responses might be, and encourages everyone to exchange responses or share in expressing a response freely. As students work together, they modify their individuality where it seems appropriate and retain it where it seems appropriate. They come to see where their language can connect them or divide them. As students work together, they find out about other people and about themselves. The teacher's role is to challenge students to justify, explain, and share their responses.

The aim of the curriculum is to have students come to a greater knowledge of why they are who they are and to approach new works of literature with greater self-confidence.

The aim of the curriculum is to affect students' perceptions of works of art (literary works), to improve their ability to articulate their responses, to increase their tolerance of the diversity of human responses to similar objects, and to bring them together into a community of communities.

What About Teaching LITERATURE?
What About All the Information That People Have to Have to Really Know a Poem or a Story?

In one sense, all the information people really have to have is in the words and structure of words of the text. There are necessary terms—*story, poem, word, repetition, scene, pattern, narrator* or *speaker, comparison.* There are many terms—*metaphor, symbol, plot, irony, rhyme, rhythm, voice, point of view, allegory*—that are useful to talk about a text. And there are a lot of terms—*metonymy, anacrusis, iamb, sonnet, heroic couplet, bildungsroman, litotes,* and *romantic irony* that belong to the specialist and become a part of his jargon but are unnecessary for most people.

The situation is just like that in any field: the same thing can be a *pitch* or a *reverse knuckle ball;* the same thing can be a *leap* or a *jeté;* the same thing can be a *layer cake* or a *kaiser torte.* One term is more precise than the other, but either is sufficient for most communication, particularly when the people talking about the thing are trying to understand each other as well as the thing.

The critical language that developed came from people's need to classify and categorize their experiences. It came from the same impetus that has led to the elaborate classifications of plant and animal life. In one sense, education is the learning of these classificatory schemes, but too often the learning of the names of plants has replaced looking at them, smelling them, enjoying them. The same thing happened to the teaching of literature.

In a response-centered curriculum, the central focus is the experience of the reader with the text. In order to ensure that this focus remains central, the learning of classificatory terms and critical descriptors needs to move from a central to a supporting role.

History and Authors and Background Help with Some Writers More than Others

Does it help your understanding of "The Pit and the Pendulum" to know that Poe drank? How about to know he loved the Middle Ages?

Does it affect your judgment of "Jabberwocky" to know that Lewis Carroll's real name was Dodgson? What about knowing he was a logician?

Does it affect your interest in Tom and Becky in the cave to know that Mark Twain was a staunch atheist? How about to know he grew up a mile from that cave?

In fact, does it affect your understanding, appreciation, interpretation, judgment, or involvement to know whether *The Tempest* should properly be called a romance or a tragicomedy? What of knowing about the Elizabethan belief in order?

Of course it does, and of course it does not. There is a time for some information, and that is the time when people are in training to be literary critics, literary historians, literature teachers, or quiz-show question writers. It is not the time when people are learning how best to express what has happened when they meet with "The Pit and the Pendulum," "Jabberwocky," *Tom Sawyer,* or *The Tempest.* The second bits of information can help some readers.

What of all that information about the author, the history of the work, or the fact that drama started as religious ritual, or the specific references to English politics in *Gulliver's Travels*? Yes, that affects a person's response; it may even lead to a kind of response different from the one a person would have reading the work without any such information. Is one response the better for having all this information? No. Nor worse. The two responses are different.

One of the problems with the teaching of literature is that all this sort of information seems to crowd the reader's response to the text out of the picture. The students get everything but the work. In some countries, literature classes consist of almost nothing except reading literary histories. The students don't read the things the histories are about, just as in some college classes in this country they read the theorists and critics, not poems and novels. In part this happens because it's much easier to make up a test of factual knowledge than it is to evaluate a response-centered curriculum—or even an analytic curriculum.

Be that as it may, background information should be precisely what it is—"background." At times it should be so far back it is out of sight. But don't deny it to those who want it.

But What Does The Response-Centered Curriculum Say About Selections, What the Students Should Read? You Seem to Have Forgotten That.

No we haven't. Remember the first chapter.

In one sense, it does not particularly matter what selections you choose. As we see it, you have two obligations: to introduce the students to works they might never read on their own, and to works that embody the variety of the cultures of the world. It's okay to have a year of American Lit. Just don't forget that the Americas include Canadians, Mexicans, Orientals, Native Americans, African Americans, immigrants of all sorts, women, men, the blind, the deaf.

Many of the anthologies contain good selections, ones that students like to read and discuss—but watch out for the questions.

Go ahead and use the anthology series the district bought. You can use some of the class sets that are back in the storeroom. You might even use a picture book and perhaps even a Nancy Drew at some point. Don't forget comics, TV tie-ins, "as-told-to books," even an adolescent lit book. Just don't make a steady diet of any of these.

We have found that students will read and consider almost anything. We have found it impossible to pin down the tastes or interests of an entire class—even a class of hardcore nonreaders. Some of them are secret sci-fi buffs. Some tell you about every baseball player going. They could try John Tunis or Bernard Malamud. Others can list off all the romance writers; have they tried Emily Brontë?

Of course, there are some caveats from our experience.

Adolescents will probably not enjoy much of the fiction about the breakup of marriage; Joyce's "The Dead" is not a good selection to assign to 16-year-olds. His "Araby" is.

It would probably be as good to present Shakespeare's *Troilus and Cressida* as it would *King Lear* in a twelfth-grade class.

Adolescents will probably get more out of Franz Kafka's allegories than they will out of Thomas Mann's philosophical novels.

Try Ursula LeGuin instead of Jules Verne.

Billy Budd will probably be more successful than *Moby Dick* with a group of eleventh graders.

Shelley's political poems will probably evoke a more energetic response than will his poems about art like "To a Skylark."

e. e. cummings's exuberant language will probably gain more adherents to poetry than T. S. Eliot's measured language.

You can teach *West Side Story* with (not instead of) *Romeo and Juliet*.

Better to elicit response with Annie Dillard than with Charles Lamb.

Take Tarzan on man and nature rather than John Stuart Mill or Alfred, Lord Tennyson. But use Tennyson's mythological material.

Use modern black writers rather than Harriet Beecher Stowe.

"Bloom County" can be as effective an exponent of satire as Addison or Steele.

Best yet, try all of these and do not be bound to any preconception.

All Right, But Isn't It Important for a Student to Have
Read the Classics?

                    Yes,

                    But

Often the inclusion of the classics triggers a bad reaction. Teachers tend to
want to worship a classic and to force students to worship it too. Students
tend to see classics as "irrelevant" because they are not able to see that
there is a great degree of generalizability from the classic to their lives.
Is *Billy Budd* irrelevant because it's about sailing ships? It's also about
the problem of relating ends to means, the problem of making unpleas-
ant decisions. Those problems are relevant to the students' world—but
it is often hard to see that when you are so wrapped up in your own
world.

Teachers can present the classics well, but sometimes they need help.
Oftentimes they need to get away from the notion that teaching the classics
means revering them and teaching their old lecture notes from English 101.

Remember that Shakespeare wrote plays not classics. He was the Neil
Simon and Arthur Miller of his day. These works are to be seen and heard. If
you cannot take students to a production of *Macbeth,* have them read the
comic version, which is the complete folio text. Don't spend a lot of time
studying every word.

Remember that Swift wrote pamphlets, not classics, to get people
aroused about current issues.

Remember that Wordsworth and Coleridge wrote poems for the people.
So did Whitman, Sandburg, Frost, Hughes, and Brooks.

Remember that a "classic" is a good example of its type. "The Most
Dangerous Game" is a classic short story. *A Tale of Two Cities* is a classic
adventure novel. So is *The Third Man.* So is *Chronicle of a Death Foretold.*
So is *A Wrinkle in Time.* The classic is the work—not the author.

Many recent works have reached classic status—*A Separate Peace, To
Kill a Mockingbird, A Catcher in the Rye, Black Boy, Diary of a Young Girl,*
the Earthsea trilogy, *Arrow of Gold . . .* the list goes on. Some classics have
lost favor—the works of Kipling, Hardy, and Scott to name but three. The
list is wide.

The important thing is to try to include the best of its kind, to include
works that repay reading and thinking about: thinking about what they say
and how they say it; how the experience of reading the book takes each of us
a little bit out of ourselves for the moment and then reminds us of ourselves
in a new way when we have finished; rereading the poem in one's memory.
These are the hallmarks of a classic.

But a Lot of These Classics—Particularly the Contemporary Ones—Are the Ones That Come Up on Blacklists. What About the Censors?

That's a problem. And it cannot be wished away. For every book there is an enemy. One reason is that our society has been taught by English and reading teachers that books contain moral messages and that we should pay attention to them. People think that reading a Sherlock Holmes story will lead to disrespect of the police, that reading *Huckleberry Finn* will make one racist, that reading Hemingway will make one sexist.

We think there are some books it would be better for our students not to read. So do you. They may be books we find personally repulsive. They may be books that deal with subjects we would rather not deal with ourselves. For all sorts of reasons we make selections based on a variety of criteria. One of us would never teach Kafka's "In the Penal Colony" because the experience was more than could be borne a second time.

So there is a little of the censor in all of us. In our experience, the problem is less censors as such than it is that of forcing students to read something that some of them or some of their parents might find repugnant. We have found that most parents and citizens groups do not mind if they are told that the students can read alternative texts and that they do not have to accept what is the supposed message of the book.

To us the more serious problem is that of the censors at the publishing houses and those who "speak" for the groups that provide "guidelines" to publishers. These are the censors who do not allow teachers and communities the right of choice. To our mind the local objectors who speak against or for books out of a clear sense of conscience are preferable to those who claim to speak for upright citizens everywhere.

If you are approached by someone who is concerned about what his or her children are reading, there are a number of things you can do. The simplest is to talk to the person, listen, ask what alternatives the individual suggests. Confrontation is not necessary. It is less important that all students read a particular book than that all read and respond to something. It is not the text but the response that is paramount in the literature curriculum.

One Last Question: All This Sounds Very Nice, But So Many Students Don't Seem to Know How to Really Read a Text.

It depends upon what one means by *really read*. People often use the phrase *really read* to mean that students do not come up with their particular "reading" of a text. Students do not see the same things teachers see, and they do not see them the same way. Surely out of 500,000,000,000 responses, the teacher's response is not superior to *any* other response.

But, if one means by *really read,* that students do not pay attention to all the verbal details that produce their general responses, there is more than a grain of truth. People who respond to Picasso's *Guernica* don't pay attention to the strength and direction of the brushstrokes. Many people who respond fully to a symphony do not pay attention to what key it's in. The comment might mean people who read poems are not professionals. It may also mean they have been trained to be lazy readers who rely on teachers and multiple-choice tests.

If one means by *really read* that students don't know the procedures for doing what literary people do when they criticize texts, that is probably right. It has been our experience that students in the early years of secondary school don't know how to go about finding the theme or meaning of a story or poem. They are often asked to come up with the theme and then told that the one they selected was wrong. They have not been given the rules or procedures for theme-finding; they don't have a map for exploration.

We expect people to be highly attentive readers, though, because they read so much, and because they take twelve years of English. And they can be more attentive than we give them credit for, but they are not used to explaining all the processes by which they come to like or dislike, interpret, evaluate, or make some other summative judgment about what they have read. There remains a question as to whether they need to or not. If you let a group of people talk about a poem for an hour without directing them in any way, you will find that collectively they touch upon most of the verbal details that produce the various general impressions. There is no need to lecture them on all these details or to hold a recitation. The trick is to get them to talk.

The students may know how to *really read;* give them a chance to prove it.

CHAPTER 5

If Literature Is Exploration, What's the Territory and Who's the Guide?

We've spilled a lot of ink about students and texts and classrooms. What about teachers? What is their role?

Teachers are pivotal in the response-centered classroom:

You usually select the texts that will be read—perhaps from a list or anthology.

You choose the sequence and timing of text, discussion, writing, films, tests, drama, talk, and grade.

You choose when to divide the class into groups for reading or discussion or projects and when to bring them back together as a whole.

You provide additional information as needed.

You provide resources.

You guide the talk.

You give the feedback.

Louise Rosenblatt wrote a book titled *Literature as Exploration*. Exploration doesn't mean being lost in the woods. It means finding out about new territory for the explorer. The students are the explorers, but they need guides who help them, who warn them of dangerous swamps and alligators, who have scouted out the territory, who arrange for the food and shelter. The guide does not replace the explorer but is absolutely necessary to a successful exploration.

You Are the Guide

Don't forget these tips for being a good guide.

1. You are older than they are (sometimes bigger too).
2. You know more than they do (about the subject, that is).
3. You are also their judge and jury (but they judge you too).

You can take these tips and be a tyrant or you can use them as a proper guide—like a gardener or the director of a play. In no case are you sure of the outcome, but you are in charge and responsible for the safety of the journey.

We've found it's a mistake to pretend to be one of the "guys" with the students. Act your age and your education. You can be sympathetic and encouraging, but there's an invisible boundary—don't cross it.

Selecting the Texts

We said a lot about this in the last chapter. The only thing we would add is an admonition that a good guide never stops being curious, never stops reading. To stop reading is the curse of English teachers and the beginning of mental decay.

Anything you read—a short story in an airline magazine, the front page of the *National Inquirer*, a new novel, the latest poem, a book your own kids ask you to read, the writings of an African poet—all are potential candidates for the curriculum.

So are the neglected classics like Sir Walter Scott and Kate Chopin.

So are the books found on remainder lists or on junk shop shelves.

So are the angry and sweet voices of your youth.

They may not all be usable, but you have a sense of what the students might want to talk about or what you might want to talk about with them.

You can certainly use the selections in the anthology you've been told to teach or the list of books in the library or the class sets. Just don't worry about the teacher's guide and study questions. Use the selections, but make them yours and your students'.

Setting Up the Sequence

You have thirty-two weeks divided into four quarters and eight marking periods, four groups of thirty students and a 5-pound anthology. What's the plan?

Regardless of how that anthology is set up, we don't recommend marching through it from cover to cover. If you don't have an anthology, but rather a set of books or a list, you will have to select an order. How do you make your own sequence?

Literature courses are traditionally organized by author (usually nationally and chronologically), by genre, or by theme. Each of these is a perfectly good arrangement. Each is artificial. Each makes sense. Each may help the students answer the question *What are you studying in English this year?* American Poetry. It's nice to be studying something tangible, nicer than studying "thinking skills," or "articulating our responses," or "self-understanding." These are educational by-products, terms for curriculum people.

Real people study people, places, or things. Subjects like fractions and grammar and Shakespeare. That's the real stuff.

That's OK. Give the students something to have a handle on. Make up a sequence that has a tangibility to it. It can be poems, or black writers, or comedy, or man and nature. It can at times be a single text like *Macbeth.*

Remember that any text in a curriculum comes before and after another. You can make all sorts of connections. Some can be based on similarity, some on contrast.

You can follow *Macbeth* with Thurber's "The Macbeth Murder Mystery."

You can put *Wuthering Heights* and Georgette Heyer together.

You can pair Carl Sandburg with Langston Hughes or Robert Frost with Maxine Kumin.

You can contrast George Orwell and Aldous Huxley on the future.

You can compare the speeches of Chief Joseph and Martin Luther King, Jr.

You can follow *The Day of the Triffids* with Sylvia Plath's "Mushrooms."

You can run a sequence of love poems from the Elizabethans to e.e. cummings.

You can pair the contrasts of place in *A Tale of Two Cities* with those of time in Alan Garner's *Owl Service.*

The pairings are endless: structure, style, tone, theme, mood, characterization, author, setting, fictionality, . . .

All they require is a sense of what might be an illuminating comparison or contrast, a sequence that makes some sense, a pairing that will help students see one text in the light of another or several others that they have read before.

Dividing the Group and Bringing It Back Together

In the subsequent chapters we are going to go into various activities in depth. One thing we do want to say at this point is: It's not necessary for everyone in the class to read the same book at the same time.

At times it's good to have the entire class read and talk about the same text. At times it's good to have everyone reading a different text. At times it's good to have reading groups.

A particular text can be a good common point. Take A *Tale of Two Cities;* it's a good novel for a group to read together. It has romance and adventure. Afterwards some of the students might want to pick up another novel by Dickens. Another group might want to follow up with some history and might look at Thomas Paine. Still another might ask if there are other novels on the French Revolution; they could read *The Scarlet Pimpernel.* Still another might ask about the Russian or American Revolution and whether it produced any fiction.

That's one way of breaking up the class into groups. After they have worked on their extended reading, they should share it with the rest of the class.

Another way of breaking up the class is to have them divide into groups to explore different facets of the selection.

In a class on Conrad's *Heart of Darkness*, after the group has read it through and perhaps had a brief discussion and found themselves baffled, you can say to them that there are a number of ways into the story they could try.

TEACHER: What might be some good leads?

STUDENT: Well, there's the journey. Where did they go?

TEACHER: Why don't three of you try to make a map diary.

STUDENT: These guys seem to be going to hell.

TEACHER: Good, know any other trip-to-hell stories?

STUDENT: I've heard of Dante.

TEACHER: The four of you in the back row look at an outline of his *Inferno* and see what you can find.

STUDENT: I'm sort of struck by *The Heart of Darkness*. There's a lot of times that comes up.

TEACHER: Why don't you and Ines and Kris make a list of all the occurrences of the term.

STUDENT: Marlowe makes a lot of comments.

TEACHER: Three of you catalogue them and see where they lead.

STUDENT: You've got two stories here, don't you?

TEACHER: Looks that way; what relationships can you find?

Without even thinking about it you have five working groups. They can report to each other and maybe some of them will come up with some rich finding. The eleventh graders that we saw do this wrote excellent papers after about two weeks of reading, digging, and articulating.

Being a Resource

Sometimes you may give a lecture or find a videotape on a background topic related to the text. You could show *Apocalypse Now* after reading Conrad's *Heart of Darkness*. Don't be afraid to tell the students something about the background if they seem to want to know it. It helps readers to have some information on Dickinson's Amherst or Jim Crow in Richard Wright's time or the fact that the Greek theater was a place for religious ceremony.

Background information can help the works come alive, but it does not replace the work. If you make a presentation, it might come after the initial reading rather than before, at the point where the addition of information clarifies potential misconception.

Just Because You Give Them Information Doesn't Mean You Have to Give Them a Test on It

We recommend having lots of adjuncts: maps and atlases for historical fiction, or fantasy. A dictionary with etymology. A history of literature. A dictionary of mythology. Photographs of art works. Diagrams of theaters and other sites. Videos concerning authors or settings. Tapes of music contemporary with the work. Many of these can be useful for clearing something up or starting a discussion.

Don't try to deny that literature has a context.

Don't try to tell students that all they need to understand a text is their native wit.

Neither is true. Don't lie to them—it's not for their own good.

The main thing you will have to do as a resource and guide is to know when to help them as they work toward an articulation of their response.

Just How Does a Teacher Program Proceed? Very Carefully (Like Those Porcupines Making Love).

You assume that the students can attend to pieces of writing by listening or reading. You know they respond, but they might have trouble expressing their response. Present something—like a story—

> . . . and wait

> > . . . and watch

> > > . . . and listen

One student waxes enthusiastic about a story that the class has just read, and says it is just lovely, you could just see everything as if it were there, and it was so moving. Another student replies, "That's baloney." Silence. *The teacher asks why each said that.* Without defending or attacking either one, the teacher asks both to be more explicit.

A student reads the passage from "The Sea" and decides to make a film. "I want to film that down at the park."

"So do I," say four others. *The teacher asks them how they would film it.* Better yet, the teacher gets a camcorder or encourages the students to get one and lets them go off and film it. Then the group can compare the film and the story and their responses to each.

Suppose a student sits stolidly, blankly, as others talk about a play. *Later the teacher asks why this student was silent.* "Didn't you like it?"

"Yeah, but I don't want to talk about it."

Be quiet. . .that time. Later, perhaps the next day, the teacher asks why the student didn't want to talk yesterday and gets a detailed explanation of the play and the initial understanding. There is no embarrassment.

Suppose a student sits quietly for a few minutes while the rest talk animatedly about a story they have read. The teacher asks why. "I don't know what you want me to say," she bursts out. *The teacher replies, "It's not what I want you to say that matters; it's my job to help you say what you want to say."*

Suppose the teacher asks students to jot down their thoughts about a story. "But it didn't involve me or interest me." "This story has no point to it." "The title is very significant." "It reads like it was written for a fourth grader." "It was boring." "The action adds flavor to the story and makes a good end." *The teacher cites these points to the class and has them talk out their differences.* Can they convince each other? How? Why or why not? What is each of them saying?

The students may remain silent; they may get up and decide to act something out; they may decide to draw, to make a film, a song medley; they may decide to hear the story again or turn to something else in the book; or they may decide to talk. And not all of them will decide to do the same thing at the same time.

The teacher must allow the students this first opportunity to express their responses. It may take a long time or a short time. It may seem dull to the teacher or seem nonintellectual or stupid or philistine. It may be exciting for the students; it's new for them, so accept what they do as genuine; listen, watch, attend to what they are doing and take notes—mental or written. Help those who want to express something express what they want to express. At the moment when you think the students have expressed their initial responses fully, ask them to clarify, to expand, to explain, to share more fully. Encourage them to ask this of each other—not to put each other down but to understand what each is doing, and why.

But What If There Is No Initial Response?

In one class, the teacher put the word *LORD* on the board and the class discussed its connotation. Next they did the same with *FLIES*. Then the teacher connected them and asked what might be implied in *Lord of the Flies*.

The discussion was long and heated. Some suggested the ruler of shit; some suggested a star outfielder; most came out with a sense of paradox. Then the teacher wrote the next words of the text:

The Call of the Conch

and the class mulled over where that phrase was taking them—away from the title? The tool of the Lord. Then they focused on the first sentence of the book for fifteen minutes. How were they being led? Where were they being led? What was the juxtaposition of two phrases and a sentence doing? The class was now open to the novel and not to some canned interpretation.

It is quite possible that the students will not know what to say. There are a number of ways to get students to begin thinking about the experience they have had reading and envisioning a new work.

Ask the students to jot down the first question that comes into their heads. Have them share the questions and see who has answers for which questions.

Have a supply of pictures that might be appropriate to the poem and ask groups to select the picture they think best illustrates the poem. Can they justify their choices?

Present students with a set of scales for the main character of a story and ask them to rate the character and share their ratings. How uniform were they?

	Low in Quality			High in Quality	
Good	1	2	3	4	5
Strong	1	2	3	4	5
Distant	1	2	3	4	5
Calm	1	2	3	4	5
Moral	1	2	3	4	5
Spineless	1	2	3	4	5
Lovable	1	2	3	4	5
Active	1	2	3	4	5

If you are reading a play, ask the class to select the actors for the dramatization and justify their choices.

Have one student read a part of the selection aloud. Then have another student pick it up. How did the two versions change the story?

Try making a drama or a choral reading of the text.

DO ANYTHING BUT DON'T TREAT IT LIKE A PASSAGE IN A READING TEST AND ASK RIGHT AWAY FOR THE THEME OR THE MAIN IDEA.

Remember the difference between "reading" a message and reading literature. Don't be fooled by the fact that reading tests include stories and poems. You are after the thoughtful articulation of the imaginative vision of a story or a poem. Cherish the experience for its own sake.

Don't look for a quick answer to a simple question like those in the teacher's guide.

Don't treat *The Old Man and the Sea* as a descriptive account of how to catch marlin, but rather the story of an old man, a boy, a fish, the sea, and their complex relationship.

Remember this is a literature curriculum, one that has its own goals and pursuits. It is not designed to get people to read reports fast or to help them answer multiple-choice questions. It is designed to help students think about their experiences, to deepen them, to challenge their assumptions. It is about literature and the culture that it forms and that formed it. It is about your students and their culture and community.

This approach to literature is to be carried through the subsequent consideration of the text. There may be a number of activities that follow from the initial experience and sharing of that experience. What follows is a sampler. Some we will explore in greater depth in the next few chapters.

Suppose that after having read Pope's *An Essay on Man* some students decide to make a collection of pictures and quotes about aspects of modern woman—a "collage" *Essay on Woman. After they have finished, the teacher asks them whether they think they have captured the movement of the poem as well as its statement.*

Suppose some students start complaining about the anthology they are using. *The teacher asks them to make up their own.* As they begin, the teacher asks them what decisions they have to make, decisions about size, type of selection, whether to have only contemporary selections, what sorts of illustrations and graphic treatment there will be.

Suppose some students decide that a poem has a really interesting beat. *The teacher asks them to demonstrate this beat, even offers the use of a tape recorder in helping them record what they mean.*

Suppose a student complains that he can't read the story. . . so he doesn't get what the class is talking about. *If it seems appropriate, after class in a conference, the teacher reads the story aloud to the student.* If other students are present in class, the teacher suggests that they dramatize the story; then all have something to respond to.

Suppose some students wonder what would happen if they had read a poem and had not known what its title was; would they have responded differently? *The teacher asks if they want to try an experiment with another class and sets up a research project that the group can carry out.*

Let's Summarize

The teacher selects much of the material because the teacher has a wider repertoire.

> The students select some too.

The teacher suggests alternate forms of response.

> If the students are talking, the teacher might suggest that they write.

The teacher structures particular forms of expressing response.

> At some points, everyone might improvise the end of a story. Even if they themselves haven't finished it, they can imagine what might happen.

The teacher structures particular modes of response.

> At some points, ask the group, "But what do you think it *means*?"

The teacher works to elicit the fullest possible response.

> At some points, the teacher must be dogged about asking "Why?" "What do you mean?" "Tell us more." "I don't understand."

The teacher calls the students' attention to certain parts of the work.

> At times the teacher may ask how a comparison, a word, a character affects what a student said. Does it change the student's response?

The teacher encourages students to be their own teachers, to teach each other.

> At times the students might suggest alternate forms of response to each other, might suggest other material. . .

The teacher encourages the students to teach the teacher.

. . . might determine modes of response, might ask each other to elaborate or check responses. . .

The teacher encourages the students to try new things.

. . . to point out parts of the work that might lead to different understandings.

Most of all, the teacher seeks to make the students aware of how much they already know, how much they already feel, how much they already understand. The teacher encourages the students to be articulate.

Being this kind of a teacher is risky—very risky. You don't know what is going to happen. You control the play but not the outcome. So come out from behind the shelter of certainty and teachers' guides. It's fun.

CHAPTER 6

"Shut Up!" He Explained: Toward a Response-Centered Community

> But I did not, in life, love Miss Duling. I was afraid of her high-arched bony nose, her eyebrows lifted in half-circles above her hooded, brilliant eyes, and of the Kentucky R's in her speech, and the long steps she took in her hightop shoes. I did nothing but fear her bearing-down authority, and did not connect this (as of course we were meant to) with our own need or desire to learn, perhaps because I already had this wish, and did not need to be driven.
>
> Eudora Welty, *One Writer's Beginnings*

In many English classrooms, teachers teach and students "student." As teachers, we stand up in front of the room and impart wisdom with great authority. Students talk when given permission and otherwise they listen (or pretend to listen) or talk to their friends or write notes or worse.

When we talk about literature we like to think we are having a conversation with our students, yet we carefully guide and monitor that conversation so as to end up at a certain point. We are concerned that what's important or significant about the story will be addressed. Important and significant to whom?

This is how some high school students describe the literature discussions in their classrooms:

> "I don't pay attention half the time. It's easier just to read the story. When the teacher explains it, she twists it all around."

> "In class discussions, we sort of have our own opinions but they get

sort of pushed aside. When the teacher focuses on something, we usually pay attention to her."

"I guess what you do is answer the questions and hopefully maybe you might express some of your feelings along with it."

We engage students in an elaborate "dance," choreographing a series of questions and answers that lead toward the "class theme." Often that dance begins with the plot, delves into character, symbolism, style perhaps, and ends with *the meaning*. Students are often amazed and somewhat relieved that the meaning, until then hidden, is uncovered by the teacher's discourse.

This discourse cycle goes something like this: The teacher asks a question, the student answers, the teacher either interrupts the answer (if it's on the "wrong" track), evaluates that answer, elaborates on the answer (to make it more correct), calls on another student, or answers it herself. Questions asked this way have been called "closed" questions. That is, classroom questions are already answered before they are asked. This type of teaching results in a recitation with the teacher as the focal point.

In 1965, William Waller described the voice in classrooms as the "didactic voice . . . the voice of authority and ennui. There is in it no emotion, no wonder, no question, no argument." (Edwards and Furlong, p. 24) Has much changed?

Here's what one student said about his experience with literature and schooling:

> In the first grade, they teach you, they ask you, "How did you like this story?" And then you tell them and you don't have to give them evidence so from second grade on they say, "I want you to give hard evidence and support your ideas," and before you know it you're writing five paragraph essays and they say, "Well, don't use your opinions in your thesis now." And gradually they allow you to use less and less of your emotions until it's not allowed. That's where we are now. I don't get any emotional reaction out of my reading anymore. All teachers want you to do is tell them how this relates to the theme they've given you. What the tests essentially say is "This is the theme, give me evidence." It's like okay that was fun. Instead of saying, "How did you feel about the story? Give examples in your answers."

The descriptions and quotes above describe particular types of interpretive communities—communities in which the interpretive authority rests with the teacher or the text or the teacher's guide. These communities often exist in secondary schools and sometimes in colleges. They are developed in elementary and middle school. These communities support a particular way of reading that is something like what the New Critics described as "close textual reading" and is sometimes called an element or academic approach to teaching literature.

> We're taught to break it down, hard and rigid: plot, theme, point of view, and all the elements of a short story.

Another kind of community supports the "main idea" approach to teaching reading; only in literature class it's the Hidden Meaning.

But how does this affect students' enjoyment of literature? What happens when students no longer have someone to tell them the theme or the Hidden Meaning?

There is no single way of reading that is correct or natural, only "ways of reading" that are extensions of community perspectives, as the critic Stanley Fish argues.

What if you went to the movies with a friend and afterward you got some dinner and your friend said: Who were the main characters? What happened in the movie? Who was the narrator?

Students learn how to read by participating in interpretive communities where people read and talk about what they read. The norms or strategies of interpretation that they learn are the ones that are directly or indirectly signalled to them through the discourse patterns of these communities. Most students are astute learners of the social rules of the classroom: when they can talk, with whom they can talk, what they can say, and how they can say it. Often it takes a week or two to "catch on" to a new teacher. Often the process can be demeaning and can hamper learning. We would like to see it ennobling and an aide to learning.

What is being signalled to students in the following example of teacher and student talk about Saki's "The Open Window"?

> T: Okay, now you can look at these two character descriptions. Can you see which one Saki is making fun of and which one he is mocking?
> S: He is elevating Vera and mocking Framton.
> T: Yes, he's definitely making fun of Framton. Saki likes to make fun of or satirize characters that think they are self-important—high society, the rich—those segments of society. So the story we have today, besides being a supernatural ghost story, is a satire.

Here is how students say discussions help them interpret literature:

> "There is usually a class theme. Everyone gets the same idea. They read the story and then the teacher will tell them what she interpreted and the class will say, 'Oh yea, that's right.' We don't really form the ideas."

> "Usually you find out what the themes are from the teacher. They have to tell you before a test."

"We all have one idea of what the theme is and that's a lot easier for the teacher also. So when she grades something, she can just say she has established the main theme."

Then What Is a Response-Centered Classroom?

In a response-centered classroom, teachers and students really listen to each other. Students have a broader range of expression, and they can even talk to each other. Feelings are shared and authority is shared. Discussions emanate from students' feelings, questions, and responses and build toward a class interpretation or several interpretations that are truly class interpretations, not just the teacher's or the one in the textbook and the one that is expected on the test. There is as much student talk as teacher talk; sometimes it seems like everyone is talking at once (sometimes it's quiet). Students explain things to each other. Students are allowed to disagree with each other and with the teacher.

In these classrooms, talk is what Douglas Barnes describes as "exploratory" rather than "final draft" talk. In exploratory talk, ideas are only half-formed and they can be revised based on what other people say and do.

This more closely reflects how people really read and talk about literature (outside of school). This might be called a response-centered interpretive community, but how does it happen?

Suppose you want to "teach" the poem "Nikki-Rosa," which follows:

NIKKI-ROSA

childhood remembrances are always a drag
if you're Black
you always remember things like living in Woodlawn
with no inside toilet
and if you become famous or something
they never talk about how happy you were to have your mother
all to yourself and
how good the water felt when you got your bath from one of those
big tubs that folk in chicago barbecue in
and somehow when you talk about home
it never gets across how much you
understood their feelings
as the whole family attended meetings about Hollydale
and even though you remember
your biographers never understand
your father's pain as he sells his stock
and another dream goes

and though you're poor it isn't poverty that
concerns you
and though they fought a lot
it isn't your father's drinking that makes any difference
but only that everybody is together and you
and your sister have happy birthdays and very good christmasses
and I really hope no white person ever has cause to write about
me because they never understand Black love is Black wealth and
they'll
probably talk about my hard childhood and never understand that
all the while I was quite happy

                                             Nikki Giovanni

After the students read it, you could ask the questions in the book that would promote a literal rereading of the poem:

What are some of the narrator's happy memories?

Or you could really kill it by getting right to the point:

Why wouldn't the narrator want a white biographer to write about her childhood?

Or you could somehow try to capture the students' feelings about the poem:

How did this poem make you feel?

Or, capture their idiosyncratic responses:

What do you think is the most significant word in the poem?

Or, find out how they responded to the writer:

What question would you like to ask the poet?

Or better yet, don't ask any questions at all. Questions somehow always get misconstrued because students are so used to assuming the teacher already has *the* answer and that they just need to guess what's in her head. We have rendered mute so many students who are afraid they will give the "wrong" answer.

Maybe before they even read the poem you could ask them to pretend the poem was sent to them as a letter, and after they read it, ask them to write back.

Here's what they might write:

Dear Nikki:

I sometimes think about my early childhood years too. All childhood memories are different. I understand what your childhood was like and even though you didn't have some of the things that other people had you had something more special; your family. Some people have everything a person would dream for but they are not happy. I think you have a lot of courage and you are not selfish at all.

Amy

I got your poem. It was very touching. When you put your childhood life down on paper you make it sound so distinct.

Heather

. . . It is very hard to say something about a poem like this.

Dan

I know that being Black is hard, for I am, but being proud of yourself makes you just like anyone else if you are happy and you know that you are being all you can be.

Sandy

I don't know how you can be so happy when your father drinks and your parents fight a lot.

Joe

If Black love is Black wealth, what is white love?

Susan

You say your childhood remembrances are always a drag, if you're Black. What were some of your memories that were such a drag? Also, what do you mean Black love is Black wealth? Please write back and explain these things to me.

Gloria

I don't think the first line of your poem needed to be put in.

Kenny

When I first read your letter I really didn't know how to react. I was deeply saddened, but then I thought you were happy. Why should I become sad reading about how you were happy? (Did you follow that?) I'm really glad you sent the letter and I'm really glad I had a chance to respond.

Adam

Dear Mrs. Giovanni:

I really can't relate to your poem, but I would like to say that I know my mother, Linda, would. The poem describes her childhood, too, from the things she has told me. . . . I wish she could get to know you. Although I didn't relate to it, I was really touched by your poem and I think my mother would be, too.

Jason

Any two or three of these letters could be discussed for a whole class period. Why is it hard to say something about a poem like this? Why did Adam feel saddened even though the poet said she was happy? Why couldn't Jason relate to it even though he knew exactly who would relate to it and why?

And what about those first two lines. Why shouldn't they be there? How are they different from the rest of the poem? And what makes Heather say that the poet's life sounds so "distinct"? How *could* she be happy when her father drank and her parents fought?

Can anyone explain to Gloria why Black love is Black wealth? and to Susan what white wealth is?

These may not be the issues you would want to discuss when teaching this poem but these are the real questions of the students. You may have wanted to discuss the juxtaposition of happy and sad images in one line or the nature of free verse. You are entitled as a member of the interpretive community to bring up your responses to students. But if they are important it is likely they will come up anyway:

"How come it doesn't rhyme? I thought poetry had to rhyme."

This is a good place to share your expertise. Students need to know about literary genres and about the analytical tools of literary study. As long as they don't replace response.

Let's listen to parts of the discussion that followed:

STUDENT: It seems like she's feeling sorry for herself at the beginning of the letter.

STUDENT: But, if she felt sorry for herself why did she say she was happy at the end?

STUDENT: Yea, If she wasn't trying to show the bad things why did she write the first two lines? That if you're black, childhood remembrances are always a drag.

STUDENT: She's saying that she's getting sick of other people feeling sorry for her.

STUDENT: She doesn't want you to feel sorry for her. She just wants you to know she had it bad in her life

. . .

. . .

STUDENT: I think she contradicts herself by saying how bad it was and that she was happy anyway.

TEACHER: Let's explore these contradictions.

STUDENT: How can someone be happy when your father drinks and your parents fight? She said she was happy, she may have been but I wouldn't have been with a drunk father and living in poverty. I wouldn't like that. It makes me realize . . . .

STUDENT: I wouldn't be happy either with a drinking father.

STUDENT: She was with people she loved and cared about. I didn't think she had a bad childhood.

STUDENT: She wanted people to know that even if you have it rough you can still be happy. Some people may not realize that.

STUDENT: I think she just wanted white people to know what her life was like, how she grew up. I don't think she wasn't trying to make people feel sorry for her. She had it sort of rough but she wasn't trying to make people feel sorry for her.

STUDENT: She liked her life. She wanted to say that you can always pull something good out of something bad. She said all the while she was happy.

STUDENT: She's saying if people would concentrate on the good instead of the bad they would see it more.

STUDENT: What would bring this to her mind to write this poem?

TEACHER: I don't know. Why do you think she wrote the poem?

STUDENT: Maybe she had something inside she wanted to get out. Maybe she had this on her mind for a long time and she thought people should know. Because when people are famous other people talk about the bad things in their life. But maybe she wanted to say she was happy.

STUDENT: She must have had it bottled up inside her.

STUDENT: She might have just written to say what it was like to grow up black. She didn't necessarily want to make a point.

TEACHER: I think you're right. We tend to assume writers write only to convey a message or a point. But that's not necessarily the case, is it?

STUDENT: It's just an expression of feeling. Her anger and frustration. To say that there were good things that happened, too.

TEACHER: What words stood out for you?

STUDENT: Black

STUDENT: Love

TEACHER: Someone asked in their letter if black love is black wealth, what's white wealth?

STUDENT: Money, money, money.

STUDENT: Health.

STUDENT: You can't live on love.

TEACHER: Who has money in our society?

STUDENTS: Movie stars, drug pushers.

TEACHER: Are these our heroes?

STUDENT: My mother is my hero. She could have left me but she didn't and she takes care of me.

TEACHER: Does anyone else have heroes close to home? A local hero?

STUDENT: My grandmother is someone I can talk to; we shop and go to lunch and we talk. She'll give me advice and I love her for it.

TEACHER: She's given you things that have no price tag.

STUDENT: I told her her letter was very touching.

TEACHER: What did you find touching about it?

STUDENT: It made me think how grateful I was because she had a bad life. But I found it depressing.

STUDENT: Why is Hollydale and Woodlawn capitalized and Chicago isn't?

STUDENT: Maybe she didn't think Chicago was as important.

When students start talking about their responses there will be natural disagreements, differing feelings, and possibly different interpretations. But there is a tendency to converge on an interpretation, too, albeit in different ways. These students seem to agree that the poem expressed frustration about misunderstandings. But they found the expression of other things, too, like love and happiness and being black and famous and the worth of money. And they noticed that it didn't rhyme and that capitalizations carried meaning.

The poem made some of them think about their own life and the people in it. And they listened to each other. Mostly.

Many things about the poem were said. Many things were left unsaid.

If you are concerned about whether students are learning about how to read and analyze literature, look again; the students discussed the following "literary aspects" of the poem:

tone

irony

structure

diction

mood

style

atmosphere

metaphor

paradox

symbolism

symbolic punctuation

They also engaged in the following "literary critical perspectives":

analysis
interpretation
generic criticism
evaluation of style
evaluation of impact
evocation
analogical reasoning

Not bad! And what did the teacher do?

Listened and recognized what was happening. Encouraged. Asked for more. Took a lot of chances.

Sounds Good. How Do I Change My Community?

If you suddenly change from one kind of community to another, students will get angry because you've changed the rules. You will have to change it carefully (like those porcupines). It will take time for them to believe that you really want to hear what they have to say. Your tests will have to change, too. But more on that later.

Here's what some students said when their community changed.

> . . . it became the students explaining it to other students instead of the teacher. . . . I thought it was good because a lot of the students have different outlooks, different points of view.

> It was a lot better, because I wasn't being graded on the teacher's interpretation because she didn't give us one. We were all kind of mad at her for not giving us one, but it may be better for us because it gives us a chance to interpret the way we want.

A good place to begin is to audio or videotape your class discussions. Listen and watch. What role do you play in the discussion? What kinds of questions do you ask? (Ones that already have an answer? What do you do if you get a different answer?) What do you do if someone doesn't raise his or her hand right away. What role do the students play? Do they try to figure out your answers or their own? Do you say something in between each student's utterance? Are you constantly evaluating student responses? Do the students ever talk to each other (about literature)? What are you signalling to students about how to read literature? Do you get a sense of how *the students* responded to the text?

This Is a Lot to Think About and Change

You could begin by thinking of other ways to stimulate discussion besides asking questions. Have them write first (Chapter 10), try using a rating scale (Chapter 5) or using visuals (Chapter 8), or plan a dramatic activity (Chapter 7), and then have a discussion. There will be plenty to talk about then.

When you do ask questions, ask ones that have no particular answer. Try not to say something right away after a student says something. And then ask the student to say more, to elaborate or clarify or explain. See if anyone else wants to respond before you do. Listen carefully.

Few things are more gratifying for a teacher than having a real and lively discussion about a good piece of literature.

> You could look at reading a poem this way: if you are thinking and there is a window nearby, you may look out—far. Your thinking will connect now and then to the scene, whenever something out there strikes your attention. Or, even more aptly, you might have a friend with you, and you would interchange, offer beginnings, slanted ideas, linked progressions. There would be a series of mental incidents, not predictable, never to be fully anticipated without the experience that comes about through following the sequence onward, point by point. Your experience would be richer—more would happen—than if you had been alone.
>
> William Stafford, pp. 5–6.

What About Other Kinds of Talk Besides Large-Group Discussions?

If you really want students to talk to each other, you can let them talk to each other in small groups (without you). Talk in small groups is likely to be productive exploratory talk, if students are cooperative and treat each other as equals and with respect.

I Heard and Read a Lot About Using Small Groups and So in the Beginning of the Year I Tried It and It Was a Disaster

Several things are important to keep in mind if you want to set up small-group discussions.

Students need to know what they are supposed to talk about in small groups (argue about an established interpretation? think of issues for the class to discuss? interview each other? talk about what would go in a computer program? work on a dramatic activity?). They also need to know what they will be expected to produce (a consensus, a list, a paper, a tableau of a scene from a story?).

They should also be able to renegotiate and reformulate those goals and procedures.

It is also useful to establish social guidelines for participating in small groups, such as: How does a student gain the floor? Under what conditions can a student interrupt another student? How can it be assured that every student will get a turn? Is one person designated a recorder, a leader? What happens when the group gets off task?

Once students know how to work together, you might suggest that they choose their own books to read and talk about just to each other. You might want to set up reading and writing "workshops" like those described by Nancie Atwell in her book *In the Middle*.

Proceed slowly and, yes, carefully.

Moving Toward a Response-Centered Community

In order to build a response-centered community, you will have to relearn how to teach and students will have to relearn how to "student." In fact, students will have to learn how to teach and teachers will have to learn how to "student." Everyone will have to learn how to talk to each other in ways that promote learning and response.

Teachers can no longer be the experts, or at least the only experts (this is not to say they can't or shouldn't share their expertise).

The class talkers will need to become listeners and the listeners talkers.

Feelings will count as much as intellect.

Literary terms can be used to scaffold and bolster responses, but not to build them.

Finally, reading inside the classroom will be a little bit more like reading outside the classroom.

CHAPTER 7

Responding Through Visual Symbols

Why Visuals?

By using visuals we can obtain student responses that we might not otherwise get through talking or writing. Visuals, as response, represent a third "sign" system through which understandings are expressed metaphorically. They provide an opportunity to express both aesthetic responses and responses to a work's form and quality, as well as to its content. In justifying the use of nonprint media as a means of representing our understanding of what we experience, some recent researchers argue that limiting the form through which we respond to literature actually inhibits what we may be able to communicate about our response. For example, although we probably would agree with Kenneth Burke that "literature is equipment for living" we also believe with Michael Cole and Helen Keysser that media, too, is equipment for living.

These two researchers argue that we actually have very little direct experience of the world—that is, "of the knowledge we have of the world very little comes from scenes in which we have literally participated. . . . Rather, much of our knowledge is obtained indirectly . . . is not immediately experienced; rather, it is constructed—it is mediated." As such, this knowledge is an "incomplete rendition of the original event" (Cole and Keysser, p. 54). Extending their arguments, we would like to suggest that using nonprint media represents an effort to extend and enrich interpretations and responses to the literature our students read, for in doing so we broaden the range of perspectives individual students may have of the knowledge they encounter in reading literature.

Semioticians such as C. S. Pierce have defined literacy as thinking in sign systems, including not only oral and written sign systems but also art, music, dance, and drama.

As Eliot Eisner argues, giving learners a choice in the form in which they are to represent their understandings (e.g., in literature) in effect gives them a choice that reflects their own conceptualizations of the world.

Okay, but. . . .

How Does This Work in an English Classroom?

In Chapter 2 we said that there would be times when students may not wish to respond in either oral or written form to a piece of literature they have just read. We have had students who have listened quietly during a discussion or sat at their desks with a piece of paper, thoroughly lost for words. However, when we gave them the option of articulating their response in another symbolic form or sign system, they became unlocked.

Suppose again that you are going to read the poem "Nikki-Rosa" (Chapter 6) but this time you decided not to talk about it or write about it. Instead, you asked students to find or create a photograph or a photographic collage that would capture their response to the poem.

Then the students might want to think about which photograph or photographic collage an author might have chosen for an illustration. Perhaps they could first discuss this in small groups, come to a decision, and then, as a large group, make a final decision, all the while explaining, arguing, and justifying.

> "I think the author would have chosen the photograph with the rocking horse and the iron fire grate because it has a sort of nostalgic feel to it. I mean, it has a sense of looking back on her past."
>
> "I think so too because it reminds you of childhood."
>
> "I like the one with the broken barbecue grill because it reminds me of poverty—everything all broken down."
>
> "But I don't think the author would have chosen the barbecue one, though, because it gives a sense of her childhood that she didn't want people to have. Poverty is not what mattered. What mattered was she was happy."

If we want students to respond genuinely to what they read, we must be careful (remember those porcupines?) not to cut off that response or to limit

Figure 7.1-1 and 7.1-2. (Photos by Terry Rogers)

it simply because we lean more toward traditional forms of responding in the literature classroom. Believe it or not, words are at times inadequate to represent how we think and feel about the literature we have experienced. Remember the last time you put down a book or left the movie theater and all you could say was "phew!" or "wow!"?

What Are Some Other Ways to Respond Through Visuals?

Whether the teacher does or does not specify the mode of visual response (and we suggest both options) the variety of possibilities in nonverbal, visual response is surprisingly extensive. We see these ranging across four possible visual dimensions:

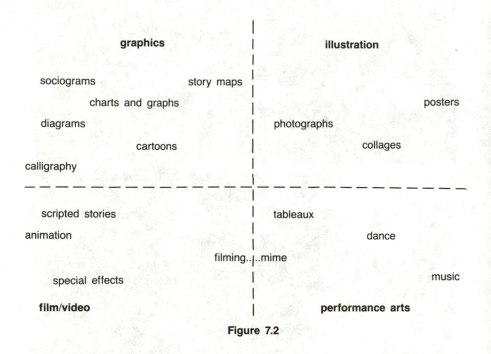

Figure 7.2

Take Tableaux, for Instance

A tableau is a "still picture" of a scene or moment from a story that is re-created by students using gesture, stance, and expression. Students can work in small groups, first deciding what scene they would like to create, then exploring different ways to represent that scene physically. When they are ready to present their tableau, it is useful to have someone count to three, at which time the tableau (or picture) is momentarily frozen for the rest of the class to view. It is fun to have other students guess what scene or moment from the story is being depicted. The following tableaux were created by students who were reading *To Kill a Mockingbird*.

Figure 7.3-1 (Photos taken by Ted Purves)

Figure 7.3-2

Figure 7.3-3

In case you couldn't guess, here are the scenes that are depicted in the tableaux.

1. The discovery of "cooties" in a student's hair;
2. The fight between Scout and Walter Cunningham in the school play-ground;
3. Atticus shoots the rabid dog, Tim Johnson.

It is useful to talk about what makes a tableau strong, dramatic, or recogniz-able. The placement of people in space, the juxtaposition of people, the suggestion of movement before or after, the shift in perspective, and the framing are all key factors.

For instance, there is enough detail in tableau 1 to recognize the scene—the teacher on the chair, a boy picking at another boy's head, and additional students looking on. The students have also framed the scene in such a way that we, too, are part of it, albeit as onlookers.

The second tableau is suggestive to us of the intensity of the physical action—the fight. Simultaneously, the figures are frozen yet dynamic because of the hunched shoulders, the bunched fists, and the coiled postures.

The third tableau has some interesting characteristics such as the depic-tion of Atticus carefully aiming the gun at Tim Johnson. Yet, Tim Johnson (the dog) is not entirely convincing and the onlookers do not portray the combination of fear and horror that were described in the book. It's useful to remember that such portrayals may not always resemble "finished" or pol-ished presentations because of the relative, yet necessary, spontaneity in-volved. However, we're not advocating perfect presentations—we are advocating involvement, discussion, reflection, revision.

It is also interesting to talk about why certain scenes were chosen (e.g., their centrality to the story, their visual quality, or their emotional quality). We have found that students particularly enjoy creating tableaux because they can actually get out of their seats using some of that bursting energy we referred to in Chapter 2 and because of the immediacy of the experience.

Story Maps and Sociograms

Story Maps

Story maps are simply illustrations of the terrain of the story, or a map of the characters' travels (e.g., Gulliver's). But their value is greater than the word "simply" implies. Creating maps of stories, poems, and plays can enhance students' understanding of the twists and turns of complex plots and calls for a close reading, which is not always a bad thing after all.

Some writers such as J.R.R. Tolkien provide their own maps:

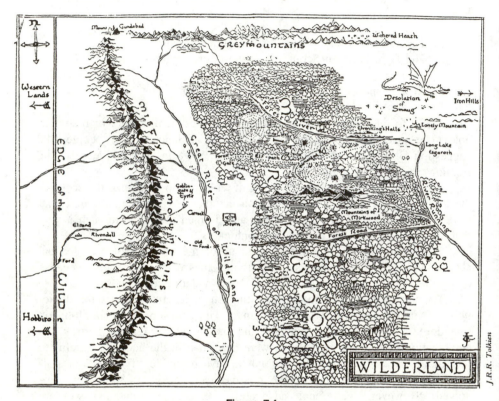

Figure 7.4

Stories that might similarly be illustrated by students are *Huckleberry Finn* and *Great Expectations* or the historical novels of Rosemary Sutcliffe. Or the *Clan of the Cave Bear*, or . . . .

Sociograms

Literary sociograms are visual displays of characters' relationships. We feel that adolescents are particularly interested in social relationships between characters and the place of individual characters in the larger social framework of a literary work. Sociograms provide a useful tool for expressing character relationships in visual form. For instance, fairly simple sociograms of *West Side Story* might look like Figure 7.5.

To do a sociogram, a student will need to think about the central characters and their alignments with each other and with minor characters. Additionally, it can make visible the minor characters and their role in the action, such as depicted in the next two sociograms.

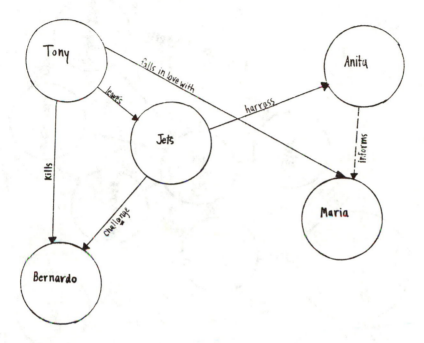

Figure 7.5

Sociograms can also be effectively used to compare modern versions of literary works with their original classic dramas. For example, we've included a student-drawn sociogram of *Romeo and Juliet* to compare with the set above for *West Side Story*.

It's particularly interesting to note the visual parallels in relationships as depicted in Sociograms 7.6 and 7.7 (*West Side Story*) and Sociogram 7.8 (*Romeo and Juliet*). As we discuss later in this chapter, these visual products can be ends in themselves or function as stimuli for more extensive exploration in, say, a literary essay.

Film and Video

Film and video are another means of articulating a response to what is read. Students should be encouraged to create film or video versions representing their responses to literature.

Over the past century, during which time films have become a staple of the artistic fare of the world, many films have dealt with literary topics. Countless novels and short stories have been made into films and a large number of plays have also had their movie versions, either directly or a live performance or through a distinctive filmed production.

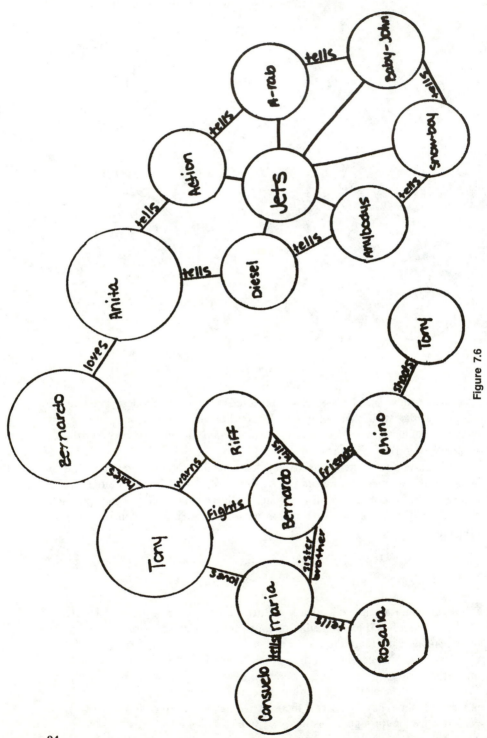

Figure 7.6

94

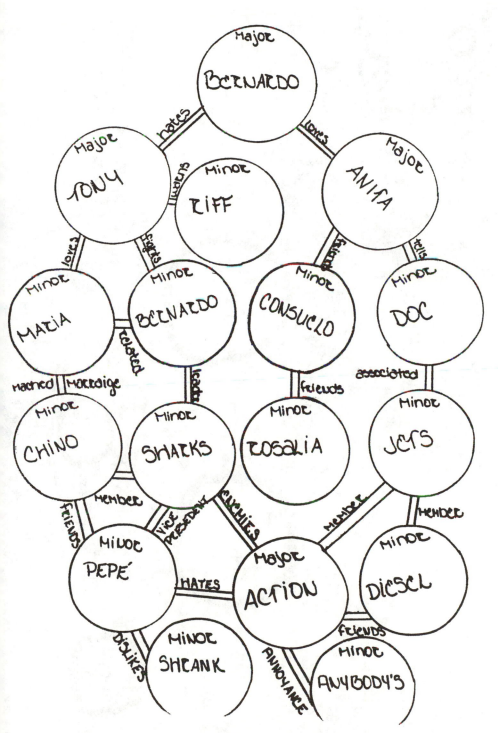

Figure 7.7

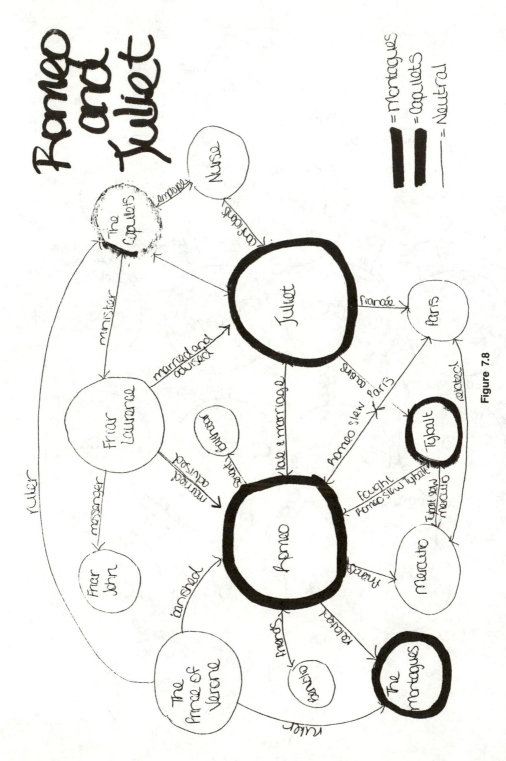

Figure 7.8

Films are captured dramas. People in the theater will tell you that theater is a living art in that no two performances are the same. Film takes one performance or an amalgam of several episodes and turns it into a distinct fixed form.

At the same time, film uses most of the devices of narrative and drama as well as certain devices that we tend to associate with poetry. Most films have plots and characters and settings, rising actions and climaxes. Most have episodes or scenes that are structured so as to make a whole. Many films will use a particular image as a motif to establish mood or to signal a type of character. The image can be visual or it can be aural, as in the use of a particular bit of theme music.

Films are perhaps more like novels than they are like plays in that the camera serves as the narrator. Film establishes how the viewer will see a scene or a character. The camera can both hide things from view and reveal them. The camera and the director are clearly central to a film much like the narrator and the author of a story or novel.

Key to the camera's manipulation of what you see are the following:

Angle. This is the relationship of the camera to the object. It can be below, above, oblique, or dead-on to the object, which may or may not be in motion. The angle may also be wide or narrow depending upon the lens used so that one may get a limited or expansive view.

Distance. The object may appear far away or extremely close to the camera (a "close-up").

Focus. The camera may bring one object into sharp focus and blur the background or it may put soft or hard focus on all objects.

Position. The camera may remain fixed in one point or it may move with the characters or move around the characters or the entire scene. This last is known as a panorama or "pan" shot.

Motion. The film may also be manipulated so that the number of frames seen per second can shift. This manipulation can make the movement of objects or people seem faster or slower than would normally be observed.

If the camera can manipulate the audience's view, so too can the director by editing the film to sequence the various frames.

Shot. What takes place from the moment the camera is turned on until it is turned off.

Scene. A series of related and connected shots usually involving the same locale or characters.

Sequence. A group of related scenes, perhaps in a given time or a given place.

The director can also affect the transition from one scene to another by use of one of the following:

Cut. A straightforward switch from one shot to another without any transition.

Fade. A gradual darkening of one shot to total blackness and then an opening into the light of the next shot.

Dissolve. Without any darkening of the scene, a "melting" of one scene or sequence into another.

These devices clearly affect what the mind of the viewer responds to, just as the various linguistic and rhetorical devices of imagery, diction, structure, and tone in a novel or short story affect the reader's response. A great deal of modern fiction has been influenced by film. Novels like Kundera's *The Incredible Lightness of Being,* Morrison's *Beloved,* Kennedy's *Ironweed,* or Marquez's *One Hundred Years of Solitude* clearly show the influence of film in their organization and sequencing of scenes. In fact, these books lend themselves easily to film treatment for that very reason.

It seems to us clear that it is important to include film in the literature classroom and that film should be studied as an art form in its own right. Studying film and examining students' responses to film is to acknowledge both the legitimacy of the form and the interplay of film and literature in the twentieth century. We show our students Zeffirelli's *Romeo and Juliet* not as an illustration of Shakespeare but as an interpretation of the play, and as a work in its own right that is designed to engage us in its own artistry. If we had time, we would also show other film treatments such as the old Orson Welles version, or the Bugs Bunny parody.

We would not limit ourselves to films of Shakespeare or other "classics"; we might well take up certain classic films in their own right, films like *The Red Balloon, Citizen Kane, Sleeper,* or *High Noon.*

What this means is that the filmed version cannot be used as a substitute for teaching. It becomes a literary work in its own right, something that provokes a response and that is worthy of discussion and study on its own. It might be compared with the text or "read" version. If such comparison is made, the point of the comparison is not to establish the superiority of the text to the film.

If we were to have a unit on the American dream, one of the texts we would certainly include is *The Wizard of Oz.* To us, that novel with its depiction of the Emerald City and the glitter and glamour of the strange world as being nothing compared to the values of home and family—and with its vision of the power of innocence to conquer evil—is the "great American novel." We would want our students to read the original, and we would also show them the film. The film takes this view and makes it even more an interpretation typical of the Great Depression. Film writers have also chosen to make it a dream rather than a fantasy. What does this shift do? Why is it important to have the same characters appear in both worlds only to be transformed in Oz? These changes also create a different experience from the book, but they do not make the film inferior to it.

Film belongs in the literature classroom. It should not be reserved for the dull days or the slow classes. It deserves respect and respectable treatment.

Film and video should be used as one of the means of articulating a response to what is read or watched. The students should be encouraged to make film or video versions of what they have read.

If, as we have argued, film is a respectable medium, film is also a respectable and interesting way to allow students to articulate their responses to the text they are reading. The film does not have to be "Oscar" material, but it should represent an understanding or environment of the text. The point of the film, like the point of dramatization, is to effect a coherent interpretation of the text. What we are proposing used to be quite difficult with the more cumbersome Super-8 movie cameras or half-inch video recorders. The activity is easier with a camcorder and cassette. We use the term "film" as a generic one even though the actual medium is not film but often tape.

Making the film involves a number of steps:

Selecting the text to be filmed

Choosing an approach

Preparing a script

Preparing a shooting script

Selecting a location

Casting

Rehearsing

Shooting

Editing

Showing

We have found that this entire activity takes about two weeks with a group. The hardest steps are the first ones: selecting the text and the approach and then preparing both a script and a shooting script, which contains the precise instructions to the camera operator. The actual run-through and shooting are not too difficult, and there are many cases in which the planned sequence is changed because of the special opportunity of the locale or the day. Editing is somewhat hard without special training, but there is often a student who has the expertise. The viewing is often a revelation for those who have made the film because they realize that what they had intended might not be the same as the effect they get, particularly when laughter comes when there should be chills.

On several occasions we have had two different groups in a class making "rival" films of the same story. One class did two versions of a Damon Runyon tale, "Butch Minds the Baby," in which a safecracker takes his baby along on a "job." The class was undecided as to whether the story should be done with Butch or the other crooks as the central character; they tried both versions. Executing the two versions simultaneously was a somewhat hectic procedure, but it was effective in allowing the class to compare the interpretations and their realizations. The comparison was not on the basis of the quality of the film or the acting, but on what they had done with the characters and what the effect of switching the focus was on the impact of the story. When the class showed the film to another class, the controversy raged all over again, but it was worth it for everyone. The students in both classes realized what the shift could do.

They learned something about point-of-view and literary techniques as well.

They also learned something about the art of film.

If you don't have the equipment to go through the entire procedure of filming a text, you can go as far as the shooting script with a class. The main point to make with and about the film version is that it is sequential— one image follows another in time. The viewer cannot go back as the reader can or even as the person looking at a comic strip can. Will Eisner refers to comics as "sequential art" and gives a bravura demonstration of how the comic artist can manipulate the reader. This is what the film can do as well—perhaps better, because the viewer is the captive of the filmmaker. That is a lesson for your students to learn. Knowing it helps them to realize that the media do indeed manipulate them unless they are aware of how they are being manipulated.

One of the most talented producers of children's films, Morton Schindel, has consistently argued Weston Wood's concern for the artistic perspective in film and its educational importance. Schindel once wrote:

> If we keep our eyes open and our imaginations free, we can choose whatever means will work best for us and for the new generation we are entrusted to educate. We can examine impartially all the media in selecting the idea we want to transmit . . . with a realistic view of the role and value of books, we can comfortably begin an exciting romance with the "newcomers" (i.e., film or video) in town—the new media—to derive ever greater satisfaction from professional endeavors.
>
> (Morton Schindel, "Confessions of a Book Fiend," in *School Library Journal,* 1967)

The illustion of unlimited space is demonstrated by the eliminaton of a panel outline.

Three small panels contained by a thick outline superimposed over a broader panel with a thin outline is meant to convey a time-focus necessary to the narrative.

The absence of a panel outline here narrates the duration of time and the limitless locale critical to the story.

The hard outline of the last frame announces the close of the sequence.

But Is All This Responding Through Images Legitimate? And Why Bother?

Is it really the province of English teachers to concern themselves with such antics? After all, literature is founded on words.

Ultimately, we think that English teachers will want to have students express responses in some verbal form and that the English classroom is an appropriate place in which to expect this. However, let's recall one of the main stated objectives of English teachers—to have students love and appreciate literature. If this is our ultimate goal it won't be well served by limiting how our students may respond to what we want them to love and appreciate.

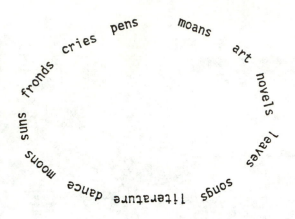

as well as liberators

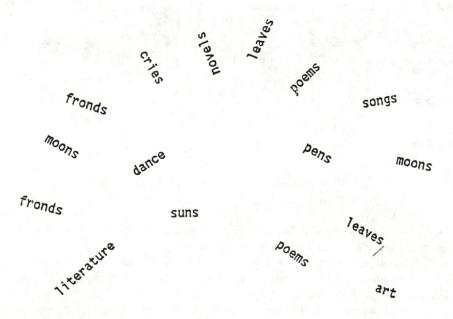

Words alone can become shackles as at least one dramatist (Samuel Beckett) realized when he turned to mime in preference to verbal drama.

We have been particularly intrigued with the nonverbal or visual response because we've realized that even quite literate college students show a surprisingly high proportion of preferences for nonverbal symbolic action in response to literature. Recently we tried the idea out again with a class of twenty-eight preservice English teachers, having them read a prose description of the making of dandelion wine. Many of them (at least 50 percent) preferred nonverbal modes of response including performance acts (such as dance and mime), creating a drawing, using a camera, making a film; of those who preferred verbal responses, only four chose the essay form.

Recent research in how we learn indicates that individual learning styles have a significant impact on how effectively we learn and on our motivation to learn. We believe that allowing students to express visual responses to literature will enhance their responses in writing and talking, rather than hinder them, and should not, therefore, be seen as simply giving them "fun" times that we (and they) don't take seriously.

Bridges to Verbal Responses

As we suggested, people have their own preferred media for expressing what they know, but we also acknowledged that one of the tasks of the English teacher is to help students communicate effectively their responses in both writing and speech. Let's concentrate for a moment on the ways in which nonverbal responses can be utilized as bridges toward effective written responses.

Recall again those students who have sat at their desks for twenty or more minutes, having written not a word on their paper. We know they read the book or poem and we may have even heard them say something in class. But the pen is dead.

We happen to know that a student (Martha) is a superb painter and sketch artist. Let's give her the opportunity to present what she responds to in the poem through her natural preferences for representing what she thinks and feels. Martha comes in with a sketch the next day, instead of a journal entry. But you really want everyone in the class to write an essay about the poem, and the journal entry was an early step in doing this. The sketch seems even more removed from the ultimate goal you had in mind. So, what's the link-up?

What we know about writing now enables us to suggest that *any* activity that promotes thinking about a topic as a precursor to writing and *any* activity that promotes articulation of that thought fosters further thoughts. At some point, students who have written an expressive response to a poem,

using their own personal language and perhaps giving little thought to "structure" in what they are writing, will have to translate these words into another
style or into another form.

Visual responses can have a similar function of "unlocking" thoughts
and feelings in response to literature, enabling us to stand back from the
work itself and, furthermore, allowing us to develop a sense of what we have
not yet seen or an angle we didn't consider. At the same time, we were also
permitted to express with dignity what we in fact did feel and think. Our
response did not have to die before it ever emerged.

Do we grade visual responses? If so, what criteria do we use? What
about students who just don't ever make the grade in verbal responses but
can do wonderful things in a visual medium?

To answer these questions, we'll first have to answer another. What are
we actually "grading" in literature study? The understanding and appreciation
of the literature itself (i.e., the response) or the form in which this understanding is presented? We believe that the answer to this question and the
answers to the preceding ones have to be aligned with our goals in teaching
literature in the first place. If we have to grade, then the focus should be on
the process and quality of perception not on the product itself. For a detailed
discussion of assessment and evaluation, we refer you to Chapter 11 but
leave you with this one thought:

> A body of research is accumulating to show that when a task can be
> enjoyable, . . . providing rewards for completing the task has detrimental
> effects on the learner's motivation to continue with that type of activity
> when the rewards are no longer offered. When the emphasis is on being
> rewarded for doing the task, the learner's attention becomes geared to
> mechanical procedures and their enjoyment of it wanes: it becomes an
> onerous chore.
>
> Brian Johnston, *Assessing English* (p. 6).

CHAPTER 8

Dramatic Response
and Oral Interpretation

Drama?

> Do you mean we are going down to the auditorium and are going to put
> on costumes and grease paint and put on a play?
> Do you mean we are going to pretend to be a tree?
> Oh, you mean readers' theater.

Drama can mean many different things to different people. The kind of
"drama in education" we are talking about takes place in the classroom, it is
largely unrehearsed, students and the teacher usually role-play real people,
and it is not "theater"; that is, it is informal and without actor/audience
separation. It draws on students' natural abilities to pretend, role-play, make-
believe.

This kind of drama does not require a script.

Okay, But What Does All This Have to Do With
Responding to Literature, Anyway?

Let's start with an example. (It is one we learned from Cecily O'Neill, one
of the co-authors of a useful guide, *Drama Structures*.)

Suppose you and your class are reading *To Kill a Mockingbird*. You
would like your students to really feel what it is like to live in the town of
Maycomb; to experience what kind of people live there.

You might start by explaining that you want to do something that will help students get a little bit more "inside" the story; that they won't be asked to perform but that they will be asked to pretend a little. Then divide them into pairs (one is A and the other is B; or if you want groups of three, then one is A and two are B's). Then you might talk for a few minutes with the students about what it was like in a small Southern town in the 1930s. Ask the B's to pretend they are a person in Maycomb. Not necessarily a named character such as Miss Maudie or Miss Stephanie or Scout, but anyone who might live in the town. A postal clerk, a barber, a child; whoever might have a perspective on what is happening in the town.

Then ask them to imagine that you are a 1930's radio producer and you would like to do a documentary on small-town life in the South. Ask the A's to pretend you have hired them as reporters to gather information for the documentary. Explain that you need some very good reporters and talk about what skills they will need to capture the spirit of a town like Maycomb (how to speak naturally with the people, make them comfortable, dig up a story, etc.).

Oftentimes it is more interesting to take on a point of view in the role you are playing. For instance, as a producer you might want a "nice" (i.e., censored) portrait of the town—nothing sensationalist—which will likely set you up for an interesting discussion or reflection session later.

Give the students time to interview and be interviewed. They may want to take notes. Walk around and give support for their interactions as reporter and townsperson as needed.

You might want to meet again with the reporters first, asking them to come to the center of the room while the townspeople listen in from the back of the room. Ask them what they learned from their interviews. They probably have heard about

A mad dog named Tim Johnson who had to be shot.

The strange Radley family.

The first snowfall in fifty years.

A schoolteacher who doesn't want her students to know how to read before they come to school.

A fire.

And, of course, the impending trial.

If you are true to your role, you will insist that the story about a supposed rape and a white lawyer defending a Negro is too sensationalist to put in the documentary. You want a "nice" documentary about a small and quiet Southern town. This should provoke discussion in role or perhaps out of role when you are done.

Next, you may want to explore the townspeople's perspective. In order to do that you might want to change your role to that of a person in the town, a leading citizen perhaps or just a milkman or businessman. Perhaps you want to meet with the townspeople at a town meeting after church to discuss these strange interviewers gadding about town. You may want to ask the townspeople what kinds of questions they've been asked. And they might tell you they have been asked about

> Their families; the children and grandchildren and husbands.
> What they do with their time.
> What it's like to live in the town.
> The fire.
> The dog.
> And the trial.

You might want to challenge the townspeople. In our classroom, the teacher in role said:

> "You didn't tell them about the trial, did you? I don't know what's gotten into that Atticus to defend a Negro, a respected member of society like he was . . ."

And a "townsperson" (student) responded in a slightly Southern accent:

> "And still is. I think Atticus has a right to defend who he wants. In all my years I've never seen the difference between a white man and a Negro, anyway."

And the town leader replied:

> "And it's just this sort of thing that's splitting up this town . . ."

And the townsperson responded:

> "Well, I'll just leave then if that's how you feel" (and she "left"—in the dramatic sense).

And for that moment, it seemed as though we were really there in Maycomb.
And what does this kind of dramatic activity do? It allows students to get inside the story in a tangible way. It might give them new perspectives on the story.

For instance, one student said, "As a townsperson I agreed with the town leader, but as me I didn't."

> Learning in drama is basically a reframing. What knowledge a pupil has is placed in a new perspective. To take on a role is to detach oneself from what is implicitly understood and to blur temporarily the edges of a given world . . . . The ambivalent position between fiction and reality is what creates drama's potency. Attempts by teachers to set up drama as a piece of real life to be lived through is to misunderstand drama. On the other hand, attempts by teachers merely to train children to be performers misses drama's potential for significant learning.
>
> Gavin Bolton

What do the students think of it?

> "Before a story was just a story, but with drama it became like real life. . . . It's not only that you're reading the story but you're participating in it, like you're in the story. . . . They're writing about you or you're in it. It makes it a lot more fun."
>
> "It helps us to see the situation from the characters' point of view."
>
> "It's like I was right in the town."
>
> "I am surprised I liked it. I thought that I'd have to get up in front of the class—the groups were better in the sense that everyone was focusing on the same topic. And I also thought that one had to be very creative."
>
> "I didn't think I'd like dramatic activities, but now I'd rather have dramatic activities than regular class."

According to Cecily O'Neill and Alan Lambert (*Drama Structures*), in order to do drama in the classroom, students must be able to

> Make-believe with regard to actions and objects.
>
> Adopt a role.
>
> Maintain the dramatic context (the make-believe) and interact with the rest of the group in a cooperative (not competitive) way.
>
> Understand and accept the rules of the game. (Sometimes you will have to make the rules more explicit: How did you feel about me as a documentary producer? You're allowed to tell me.) (pp. 11–12)

According to Dorothy Heathcote, who pioneered this approach to drama in the classroom, the "mantle of the expert system of teaching involves a reversal of the conventional teacher-student role relationship in which the students draw on the knowledge and expertise of the teacher . . . the teacher assumes a fictional role which places the student in the position of being the 'one who knows'."[1]

That is, the dramatic context provides a way for students to discover what *they* know about the story, about their feelings and responses, and about the world.

As one teacher said:

"If I stood up in front of the room and tried to tell them to feel the way a certain character felt, it wouldn't have done any good. But when they role-played the part, when they turned into a local townsperson, when they became, say, Stephanie Crawford, then they knew what she felt like."

But I'm Not a Drama Teacher

You don't have to be. All you need is a little imagination, a willingness to take risks in front of your students, and some practice. Some theatrical skills are handy, but you will develop some as you go along. For instance, you will learn to be more convincing in role without overacting.

You will develop some "directing" skills, too. You will learn to structure the drama from the inside. You will figure out what to do if it's not "working"—if no dramatic context is being built. Do the students know who they are? Is there something interesting to interact about? Are they listening to each other? It's all right to go out of role to redirect or regroup, and then go back in. O'Neill and Lambert also offer these guidelines:

Move the pupils into the drama quickly and economically by inviting an immediate response to the role.

Present the kind of challenge which may help to focus the pupils' thinking and lead them into a more concerned involvement with the context of the enquiry.

Provide a model for the pupils' contributions by demonstrating appropriate language, attitudes, action, and commitment.

Offer encouragement and support through [your] own involvement.

O'Neill and Lambert, *Drama Structures*, pp. 21–22.

In role, the teacher can be an actual listener, not an evaluator, and thus has a whole new range of communication strategies open to him or her. The

---

[1] D. Heathcote, and Phyl Herbert, "A Drama of learning: Mantle of the expert." *Theory into Practice* 24 (1985), pp. 173.

teacher can operate through a wide spectrum of roles, as well as using the traditional teacher options of instructor, narrator, side coach.

David Booth, "Talking in Role, Thinking for Life," in *Drama Contact*, p. 10.

But What Are They Learning?

The discussions or reflection sessions you have during the dramatic activities or afterward provide an opportunity to discuss what happened, to explore what the students have learned about the events, the characters' personalities and feelings and relationships, and about the issues or themes in the story (such as loyalty and prejudice). Students will better understand what happened and why it happened, the characters' motivations, and even why the world was or is the way it is.

> "The town meeting helped me the most to understand *To Kill a Mockingbird*. It kind of gave me a picture in my mind of the people and the town and a better understanding of why things were what they were in that town."
>
> "It helped me understand the people and why they did certain things."

And they will see how the other students interpreted the work:

> "The town meeting helped me because I got other people's views of the characters."
>
> "I found that other people had found things in the story that I didn't and vice versa."

They are also learning how to talk to each other, how to ask each other questions, and to listen carefully and contribute to the drama in appropriate ways. And they enjoy it.

> "It was fun because you could use your imagination."

And how often do students use their imagination in school? How often do they use their imagination to respond to and interpret literature? How often do they have fun?

Dramatic activities also provide a stimulus and a focus to many different genres and functions of writing. We have found that it also gives voice to students' writing, a voice that we don't otherwise see or hear.

For instance, after the dramatic activity we described, students may want to write a diary entry as Calpurnia, or Scout, or Boo Radley. Maybe it would be written many years later. Here is one example:

Dear Diary–

Today waz a horibl day. Mistur Finch cam hom durin the Misonary Society meetin and I new somethin waz wrong cause he never comes hom durin the meetins. He cam in the kitchen and told me Tom had been killed while tryin to escape. Shot 17 times. I dont beleve them prizon guards. Tom wood never tri to escape nowin Atticus was trin his best to get him out. I just felt so bad when I had ta tell Mz. Robinson the news. I think it waz the worst thing I ever told anyone. When we got to ther house I didnt even hav to say anything. She droped to the ground lik a sak of potatas. Ill never forget thiz day for the rest of my life.

Yours truly,
Cal

They may want to create a dialogue between two (or more) characters in town.

They may want to write up that documentary.

Or, create a town newspaper as did the students we worked with.

The Maycomb Times
Guilty or Innocent?

Negro Tom Robinson has been accused of raping local nineteen-year-old Mayella Ewell. Sheriff Heck Tate describes her condition as severely beaten on the right side of her face with fingerlike bruises around her neck.

Robert Ewell, Mayella's father, claims that while he was carrying fire-wood back to the house he heard screaming and saw Robinson run off. Mayella said she asked Robinson to come in and help her chop up a chiffarobe for a nickel and when he came inside he tried to take advantage of her.

Link Deas, Robinson's employer, exclaimed, "I've never had a better worker in my life. Tom's been with me for eight years and I can't see him doing anything like that." Robinson had no comment.

The trial is this Saturday and Robinson will be defended by Atticus Finch.

Maycomb Unites to Put Out Blaze

A fire raged through the home of Miss Maudie Atkinson on Thursday, November 28th, at around 3:00 A.M. The fire was determined to be caused by some hanging plants that caught on fire from the fireplace in Miss Maudie's dining room. Miss Maudie said she had left the fire burning all night so her plants wouldn't freeze due to the extreme low temperature.

Maycomb County's sheriff, Mr. Heck Tate, successfully warned the citizens of Maycomb about the fire with the newly purchased town alarm siren. However, the old Maycomb firetruck stalled, so help was sought from Abbotsville and Clark's Ferry, sixty miles away. When the other fire squads arrived and attached their hoses to the hydrant, the water pipes exploded.

Although the fire devoured most of the house, the men of Maycomb salvaged some of the furniture and carried it to a yard across the street. Mr. George Avery, stuck in a window while trying to escape, fell from the second story window receiving minor back injuries.

Miss Maudie was thankful and appreciated the help she received. When asked about the damage to her home, Miss Maudie replied, "I hated that old cow barn anyway. Thought of settin' fire to it myself, except they'd lock me up."

It occurred to us that without the dramatic activities, these students would not have written their newspapers with such enthusiasm and style.

Terms

Drama in education: the use of role-playing and other dramatic exercises and elements of theater that are used in an informal way to build dramatic contexts in which student knowledge is explored and extended. An approach to drama with roots in England that are largely attributed to such noteworthy experts as Dorothy Heathcote and Gavin Bolton.

Role-playing: using personal knowledge, experience, and beliefs to pretend, make-believe, and create characters and dramatic contexts.

Mantle of the expert: the notion that responsibility, knowledge, and expertise belong to whoever dons the "mantle."

Drama structure: a structured dramatic framework or series of lessons in which a dramatic context is established.

Reflection: an awareness of what is or has happened during a dramatic activity, which can be made explicit within the dramatic context (in role) or out of the dramatic context (during discussion).

Closing Thoughts

Using informal dramatic activities can be a powerful way to draw on students' own responses to a literary work, extend those responses, and build community interpretations. It is a particularly useful way to allow students to take on various perspectives and to frame or reframe their responses; it allows them (and us) to momentarily get "inside" a literary work and to see things from another perspective. Finally, dramatic activities transfer the authority for interpretations from the teacher back to the students, and they expand the forms and functions of language in the classroom. Drama is fun but it is also a powerful learning medium.

Scripted Drama and Oral Interpretation

Of course a great deal of the literature that students read is itself dramatic, and a good part of the program should encourage students to realize the dramatic potential. Drama is a form of interpretation and response. The performance of *Macbeth* is not the same as the script, just as the reader's understanding of a novel is not the same as the text. Students should be encouraged to use performance as a way of articulating their response to the text; doing so will often force them to come to a decision about how they want others to perceive the text.

That's my last duchess hanging upon the wall. . . .

If you were the Duke in Browning's poem, how would you say that line? Which word would you emphasize?

That's my last duchess hanging upon the wall . . . *Proud?*

That's *my* last duchess hanging upon the wall . . . *Possessive?*

That's my *last* duchess hanging upon the wall . . . *Anticipatory?*

That's my last *duchess* hanging upon the wall . . . *Noble?*

That's my last duchess *hanging* upon the wall . . . *Aesthetic?*

That's my last duchess hanging upon the *wall* . . . *Questioning?*

That's my last duchess hanging upon the wall . . . *Unfeeling?*

Which is right? Why not let the class decide? Then have them carry the characterization by reading through the rest of the poem. Groups could work up a set of different readings, tape them, then compare the effect.

A great deal of poetry was meant to be heard, to be shared as an oral experience. We think that nearly every poem should be read aloud. In the course of reading poems and dramas over a semester or a quarter, most students will develop an ear for the sound of different kinds of poetry. They will also begin to notice the particular effects that a given poet uses.

THE ECHOING GREEN

The Sun does arise,
And make happy the skies;
The merry bells ring
To welcome the Spring;
The skylark and thrush,
The birds of the bush,
Sing louder around
To the bells' cheerful sound,
While our sports shall be seen
On the Echoing Green.

Old John; with white hair,
Does laugh away care,
Sitting under the oak,
Among the old folk.
They laugh at our play,
And soon they all say:
"Such, such were the joys
When we all, girls and boys,
In our youth time were seen
On the Echoing Green."

Till the little ones, weary,
No more can be merry;
The sun does descend,
And our sports have an end.
Round the laps of their mothers
Many sisters and brothers,
Like birds in their nest,
Are ready for rest,
And sport no more seen
On the darkening Green.

                              William Blake

The simple seemingly happy song has small changes from stanza to stanza—which do they hear? What do the changes suggest?

DREAM VARIATION

To fling my arms wide
In some place of the sun,
To whirl and to dance
Till the white day is done.
Then rest at cool evening
Beneath a tall tree
While night comes on gently,
   Dark like me—
That is my dream!

To fling my arms wide
In the face of the sun,
Dance! Whirl! Whirl!
Till the quick day is done.
Rest at pale evening . . .
A tall, slim tree . . .
Night coming tenderly
   Black like me.

                              Langston Hughes

Are the two stanzas the same? One group could read the first and another the second at the same time. What sort of music would be a good background to the syncopation?

Of course some poems are meant to be read by more than one voice; then the students can try the pairing:

THE PHOENIX

I am Phoenix	I am Phoenix
	the fire-bird!
Phoenix	Phoenix
everlasting!	
I am Phoenix	I am Phoenix!
	Immortal
Immortal	eternal
eternal.	undying.
I live in	
Arabia	Arabia
	I'm as large as an
eagle	eagle
My feathers are	
scarlet,	
purple	scarlet,
golden.	purple.
	There is but
one	one
	Phoenix—
there have never been more.	
I am my own	I am my own
daughter	mother
granddaughter	grandmother
great-granddaughter	great-grandmother
I was	I was
	my own midwife,
will be	will be
my gravedigger.	For each time I discover
I gather up twigs of	I'm becoming old
sweet-smelling spices	sweet-smelling spices
and build a nest	
on the top of a palm.	
	I climb inside.
Then I wait for noon—	
	and when the sun's hot as fire
fire	
I flap my wings	
	till the twigs beneath me
burst	burst

into flames	
	which I fan
which I fan	with my wings
with my wings	and fan
and fan	and fan
	till the fire
and I	
	are no more.
Eight days pass.	Eight days pass.
The ashes cool.	
	Then, on the ninth day
in the morning,	
	at dawn,
just as the sun	
	rises in the east
I rise	I rise
from the ashes	
and fly upward—	
	a
new	new
	Phoenix,
my own	
mother	daughter
grandmother	granddaughter
great-grandmother	great-granddaughter
and on	
and on	and on
until the end of time.	until the end of time.

Paul Fleischman

One class that tried this began to develop a choral approach to much of the poetry. In this poem, they placed the two "voices" in counterpoint or as melody and harmony. They then moved to find poems that might be read together like the two voices in the folksong "Scarborough Fair" or the invitation and response poems of the sixteenth century.

THE PASSIONATE SHEPHERD TO HIS LOVE

Come live with me and be my love,
And we will all the pleasures prove
That valleys, groves, hills, and fields,
Woods, or steepy mountain yields.

And we will sit upon the rocks,
Seeing the shepherds feed their flocks,
By shallow rivers to whose falls
Melodious birds sing madrigals.

And I will make thee beds of roses
And a thousand fragrant posies,   10
A cap of flowers, and a kirtle
Embroidered all with leaves of myrtle;

A gown made of the finest wool
Which from our pretty lambs we pull;
Fair linèd slippers for the cold,
With buckles of the purest gold;

A belt of straw and ivy buds,
With coral clasps and amber studs;
And if these pleasures may thee move,
Come live with me, and be my love.   20

The shepherds' swains shall dance and sing
For thy delight each May morning:
If these delights thy mind may move,
Then live with me and be my love.

Christopher Marlowe

THE NYMPH'S REPLY TO THE SHEPHERD

If all the world and love were young,
And truth in every shepherd's tongue,
These pretty pleasures might me move
To live with thee and be thy love.

Time drives the flocks from field to fold
When rivers rage and rocks grow cold,
And Philomel becometh dumb;
The rest complains of cares to come.

The flowers do fade, and wanton fields
To wayward winter reckoning yields;   10
A honey tongue, a heart of gall,
Is fancy's spring, but sorrow's fall.

Thy gowns, thy shoes, thy beds of roses,
Thy cap, thy kirtle, and thy posies
Soon break, soon wither, soon forgotten,—
In folly ripe, in reason rotten.

Thy belt of straw and ivy buds,
Thy coral clasps and amber studs,
All these in me no means can move
To come to thee and be thy love.   20

But could you last and love still breed,
Had joys no date nor age no need,
Then these delights my mind might move
To live with thee and be thy love.

Sir Walter Ralegh

They tried reading this pair, alternating first the whole poem and then stanza by stanza and then line by line. They then played the recordings of each to another class. There wasn't much more to say about the poems. The readings were the best articulation of a response they could come up with. Poem after poem repays an oral reading. As the students gain experience, they show that they have learned a good deal about versification and about the tension between the way poems are set up on the page and the way they are to be read.

They lose the tendency to stop at the end of every line.

They begin to develop an ear for rhythms and meter and to read the poems as if they are poems, not bus tickets.

They begin to hear and present different voices.

They realize that by changing the voice they can control the interpretation.

They find that memorization isn't so hard and it's fun.

They realize what Robert Frost meant about "the sound of sense" in his letter of July 4, 1913 to John Bartlett. Frost wrote:

Now, it is possible to have sense without the sound of sense (as in much prose that is supposed to pass muster but makes very dull reading) and the sound of sense without sense (as in *Alice in Wonderland*, which makes anything but dull reading). The best place to get the abstract sound of sense is from voices behind a door that cuts off the words. Ask yourself how these sentences would sound without the words in which they are embodied:

> You mean to tell me you can't read?
> I said no such thing.
> Well read then.
> You're not my teacher.

Robert Frost, *Selected Letters*, ed. Lawrance Thompson. New York, Holt, Rinehart and Winston, pp. 79–80.

Some classes we have observed have taken these ideas and developed an extensive reading repertoire. The students took the readings out of the classroom and formed a group that read for various community functions. Choral reading can be as exciting and moving as choirs. It's an exciting way to present poetry.

But you don't have to go that far. Simply have the students read aloud and make the reading of the poem an aspect of the response. Sometimes the reading is all you have to have. Sometimes the students will talk about the reading. A class that read Frost's dramatic poem "Home Burial" with three voices—one for the husband, one for the wife, and one for the narrator—burst into a furious discussion of the relationship between the two characters. They were split as to whether the wife was crazy and unfaithful or whether the husband was a murderer. After a half hour they resolved the poem and tried another reading, indicating that resolution. Both characters were sympathetic, but the wife came out on top.

And Then There Are Plays

Plays are meant to be heard and seen. They are not to sit on the page and be dissected. This statement is particularly true of Shakespeare. The dialogues that he wrote slipped by the ears fast. The actors did not stop to explain a phrase or repeat a line so that an audience could get it. Much of the imagery and complex language rushed by the audience so that it was the drift and not each individual segment that was the focus. The words and lines are parts of a speech said by a character in a situation.

> The opening of *Hamlet* presents two scared soldiers half hoping they won't see a ghost.
>
> Act 3 of *Julius Caesar* shows an assassination as hurried and confused as any that might be seen on a nightly news program.
>
> Romeo and Juliet are adolescents meeting on a first date.
>
> The porter's scene in *Macbeth* presents an ordinary world that contrasts with the horror of the murder in the scene before.

What is true of Shakespeare is true of other plays that you will read with your students. They are meant to be seen and heard. The script is to help actors in their performance. That means that in class the plays should be performed. You are not going to turn your students into professional actors and you don't have to be a theatrical type to teach drama this way. But get your students out of their seats—and get off your own backside too. It won't hurt; and you could also have fun.

Reading plays means reading plays as drama. But there are a number of traps to beware, particularly since a good number of your students are not actors and you aren't aiming for production.

Take the play scene by scene with one group of students cast in each scene. Don't switch characters every page in the text.

Give students time to practice and to think about their scene. It's hard to read cold.

Work to get the students listening to each other. They may need some help in learning to avoid concentrating so much on their own lines that they forget it's a play. Have them run through the scene at least twice. Encourage the other students to suggest alternatives.

Make sure everyone gets into the act—even the ones in the back row who don't want to get involved in anything. Nobody gets out of having a part and everyone should have a chance at a substantial part. The play then becomes the property of the class.

Run through a whole scene before breaking for comment. Make sure the comments are on the characters not the students as actors. This isn't acting school; it's a literature class.

Between readings have them decide how the scene should be played—as farce or straight; with lots of emotion or not; fast or slow—these are all decisions that they will have to make. These decisions are their response to the text, and the enactment is their articulation of that response. You don't need much "literary discussion." The students have just done it.

Have the students stand when they read. It's hard to get into the part sitting like a student.

Don't take a part yourself. You can be an audience and a critic. You can also be a director. That does not mean being a dictator or forcing your interpretation. But you will have to ask your casts to agree among themselves on a consistent reading of a character.

The reading should be an enactment, one in which the students have decided something about the characters and how they might move and talk and particularly how they should relate to each other. On the basis of those decisions, they do their reading. What are the inner tensions among the conspirators as they plan to do away with Caesar? What does Willy Loman's family think of him and how do they show it or hide it? What are the changes in family relationships as we witness the characters in *A Raisin in the Sun?* The students' voices and perhaps some of their movements should work to reflect these relationships. They are an interpretation of the play. They are indeed an articulation of a response to the text.

A class that is reading Thornton Wilder's *Our Town* has to work out the characterization of Emily and George and particularly the Stage Manager. They need to come to decisions about the mood of the play. Is it optimistic or pessimistic? Is the Stage Manager a manipulator or a character on the sidelines? Is the love affair sappy? Is Emily a dumb girl or a mature woman at the end? How do each of the other characters contribute to the mood of the play and its various scenes? These are decisions that can be made during the course of enacting or reading the play. There does not have to be an elaborate production. The students don't have to "learn their lines," but in going through a readers' theater presentation of the play they will have learned their lines and they will have learned the play too.

One class we saw worked through a reading of *Death of a Salesman* over the course of two weeks. By the time they came to the end, some were in tears and most had lumps in their throats. There was no discussion. There didn't have to be. That's drama.

CHAPTER 9

Microchipping Away at Literature

English classes, and literature classes in particular, should have changed in the past decade, thanks to the introduction of the personal computer. It is our sense that this technology as well as others, except the VCR, has had a minimal impact on the literature classroom.

You will find students using word processors to write their papers. But they won't be using them with literature.

The students will know a lot more about computers than will their teachers.

"Nintendo" exists out of school. Who sees it as a form of literature?

In sum, the literature classroom has not come to terms with the electronic age. And it is odd. First of all, one must realize that the computer is in many ways like the book—or the library. It is a means of storing information and helping people retrieve and manipulate information that has been stored. That is what books are, too, of course, so that when one thinks of using computers in literature courses, the best way is to think of them as extensions and modifications of the page.

To think again about what we are after, we can see that computers have two interlocking uses: presenting literature and recording articulated responses. They can do them separately or together.

Computers can be used as a means of presenting literature. The machine can help present some texts, and preprogrammed questions and response starters are certainly viable.

The computer could also be used as a form of articulating a response by creating a computer game based on a text, by using desktop publishing, and by networking responses to a text.

These may not seem to be particularly controversial, and we do not intend them as such. We would like to advance both ideas as reasonable given the nature of technology and our students' understanding of it.

Computers Should Be Used as a Means of Presenting Literature

A few experimental programs have poems and stories available on the screen for students to read. This is not a particularly efficient means of presentation except when it is combined with another feature of the computer, namely its ability to access other information quickly. This is the feature known as "hypertext."

Typical computer technology displays one text at a time on computer screens. With the use of a "hypertext system," a student can create or access many related texts and display them on the screen, thus creating hypertext. The flow of reading, then, can be redirected from a basically linear direction to any alternative direction or flow that suits the reader's particular needs or purposes. For instance, suppose you are reading Faulkner's short story "A Rose for Emily" and you come to the part where Colonel Sartoris is mentioned and you recall that name from other Faulkner stories. Assuming a rich hypertext program for this story was already in place, you could access information related to the use of that character's name in stories such as "Barn Burning" and "The Bear." When you found the information you were seeking, you could then return to the spot in the story where you left off. Or if the name Homer (Barron) strikes you as an allusion, you could access information about the use of the name "Homer" in literature or access information about what critics have made of the symbolism of the name. Perhaps after recovering from the shock of the story's ending, you think it would be interesting to reread the story in chronological order to grasp the sequence of events that led up to that ending. Or, perhaps you are left with the question, "Did she really sleep with a corpse?" To answer this you might want to simultaneously access a sequential telling of the story and the numerous critical pieces addressing this very question.

In addition to accessing numerous types of related texts, the video laser disc technology allows you to access visual material related to the text, which can also be displayed on the screen or on a separate screen. In this case, you might want to view a particular scene from a film version of the story, or several related scenes that are not necessarily in the sequence of the story or in chronological sequence.

The potential of the hypertext and hypermedia technology is limitless. Students themselves can write hypertext programs, and depending on what information sources you link up with (e.g., libraries) there is no limit to information that can be accessed and the programs that can be developed.

The benefits of such a program in the response-centered literature classroom are clear. It supports the reader's response to a text, and it allows students to build their own understandings, environments, and interpretations of the meanings of the text. It also supports the intertextual nature of reading literature (see Chapter 3). Readers can access other works of literature by the same or other authors, other "readings" of the text, information about the author, or juxtapose one aspect of the text with another. There are a few challenges:

The user can be too dependent on the programmer's idea of what should be linked and how the links are named, students should be authors, not users.

The screen is not easy to read; students should use printouts to check the screen and see if what they see is what they want.

Preprogrammed "Teaching" of Response Articulation

As in other fields, the idea of teaching programs in literature is attractive. The only problem is that there are not many good programs that we have seen. A number of programs have treated the reading of literature as if it were "reading," with all the wrong answers and pseudo-responses—an electronic multiple-choice test.

A few programmers, particularly in England, have undertaken experimental versions of response-based programs. The options we have seen include those that allow the student to read a poem and select a response to it. In some cases the students can write a brief response; the computer can scan it for certain words and then ask the student to elaborate on those words.

Another experimental program type is one that allows the student to select one of a number of questions about a text and then trace the answers to those questions as those answers were given by other students. Still a third type of program starts with the selection of a question and then tells the student what sorts of items must be included in an answer to that question. An example of how the program would work follows:

Read the following text:

The Sea
Poor boy. He had very big ears, and when he would turn his back to the window they would become scarlet. Poor boy. He was bent over, yellow. The man who cured came by behind his glasses. "The sea," he said, "the sea, the sea." Everyone began to pack suitcases and speak of the sea. They were in a great hurry.
The boy figured that the sea was like being inside a tremendous seashell full of echoes and chants and voices that would call from afar with a long echo. He thought that the sea was tall and green, but when he arrived at the sea, he stood still. His skin, how strange it was there. "Mother," he said because he felt ashamed, "I want to see how high the sea will come on me." He who thought that the sea was tall and green, saw it white like the head of a beer—tickling him, cold on the tips of his toes.
"I am going to see how far the sea will come on me." And he walked, he walked, he walked and the sea, what a strange thing!—grew and became blue, violet. It came up to his knees. Then to his waist, to his chest, to his lips, to his eyes. Then into his ears there came a long echo and the voices that call from afar. And in his eyes all the color. Ah, yes, at last the sea was true. It was one great, immense seashell. The sea truly was tall and green.
But those on the shore didn't understand anything about anything. Above they began to cry and scream and were saying "What a pity, Lord, what a great pity."

Ana Maria Matute

Of the following questions, which one do you think is most important to ask about "The Sea"?

- What do I think the story means?
- What sort of a story is this?
- Why is this story written the way it is?
- Is this a well-written story? Is it any good?

You have selected "What does the story mean?" That's a good question. I don't know the answer to it but maybe you can tell me. First tell me which of the following clues to meaning I should pursue. Select one and then hit RETURN.

- The narrator's comments
- Contrasts and oppositions
- Sudden shifts and things put next to each other
- Repetitions of words, phrases, or images
- The title
- The character of the boy
- Symbols
- Allusions to myth or folktale

You selected "Contrasts and oppositions." That was an interesting choice. Please enter the contrasts that occur to you.
[Student enters three: *sea and land, boy and those on the shore,* and *life and death*.]

That's a good list. I've been collecting contrasts too, from other readers, and I've got several. Which of these did you think of?

- the sea and the land
- the top of the sea and under the sea
- the spectrum of colors
- the boy and the grown-ups
- the thoughts of the boy and what he saw
- the narrator and the characters

So we picked two that are the same. Please enter the others you thought of that I missed. [Here the program can add any new ones to its memory.]

You thought of all of mine and some others as well? What do you think these add up to in the way of a meaning? Hit RETURN and type your answer.

Do you want to stop here or go on to another clue? Hit RETURN to go to another set of clues. Type S and hit RETURN to stop.

Let's go back to the set of clues. Choose another, and type your response to that one.

- The narrator's comments
- Sudden shifts and things put next to each other
- Repetitions of words, phrases, or images
- The title
- The character of the boy
- Symbols
- Allusions to myth or folktale

The program can cycle the student through all the clues, or allow the student to end and summarize the meaning of the story. Each of the questions has a set of alternative avenues for the student to explore in coming up with an answer. This sort of program can be written without having the programmer estimate all of the response possibilities but allows for new ones to be added. That sort of program, involving a reading capacity, is an alternative.

As we have said, few of these types of programs exist in commercial form. There are programmed tests on some literary selections, which seem quite useful as both a testing and a teaching device, but again these are not very frequent. More often than not the programmed materials for literature are not good. We need to wait a few years. Meanwhile. . . .

The Computer Could Be Used as a Form of Articulating a Response

Perhaps the best people to work with computers and texts are your students. We have found that a number of our students who enjoy computers have experimented with creating teaching programs for other students.

Some have taken class profiles of response to a poem and used statistical packages to examine central tendency and dispersion. One way was to use the type of scale we mentioned on p. 69. In this version the scale was attached to a sonnet by Shakespeare. The teacher had divided the sonnet into four parts at the end of lines 4, 8, 12, and 14. After each break, the students were to report their ratings of the poem on a number of dimensions using a scale of 1 (low) to 5 (high): *Good, Strong, Moral, Passive, Simple, Dark, Subtle, Vigorous, Happy.* After the students had done their individual ratings, the student programmer entered the results and determined a class rating and a profile of change on each dimension. The class then discussed the results and through the discussion showed how fully they could articulate their response to and understanding of the poem.

Some of them have come up with games. Often these games are based on Dungeons and Dragons ™ or on similar war games. Others are more like board games. One of the most successful we saw was a game based on *Macbeth,* in which the central characters attempted to gain the castle at Dunsinane.

Another game based on *A Tale of Two Cities* used maps of London and Paris and had the characters move back and forth. Another student used the same concept for *Wuthering Heights.*

A third game had Huck Finn try to get down the river and escape the various people and incidents pursuing him. This one was not unlike Pac-Man.

Creation of these games showed an understanding of the story and a facile ability to create a program. Not all of the games were computerized; one senior created Pictionary ™ versions for the characters from the Greek and Elizabethan plays they read, and a junior created a black literature Trivial Pursuit ™.

The computer as a word-processor has enabled students to create their own anthologies. The desktop publishing capability of the computer allows students to explore format and layout as they put their favorite poems on disc and then create anthologies. They have been able to experiment with the use of different typefaces in presenting their text and some of them have even generated graphics to go with their text. Students have found that the context, particularly the visual context, is important.

Gray goose and gray gander, waft your wings together, and
carry the good king's daughter over the one-strand river.

> Gray goose and gray gander,
> Waft your wings together,
> And carry the good king's daughter
> Over the one-strand river.

Gray goose and gray gander,
Waft your wings together,
And carry the good king's daughter
Over the one-strand river.

Gray goose and
gray
gander,

Waft your wings

together,

And carry
the good king's daughter
Over

the   **one-strand**
                    river.

Each of these versions makes the nursery rhyme different for the reader. So too can the various versions created by the students as they make and form their anthology. They can also add illustrations, can set off dialogue differently, and re-create a text as a newspaper story.

Some students have taken Stephen Crane's "The Open Boat" and put it next to the newspaper version Crane wrote, then reset the story as if it were in newspaper columns to see the extent to which format affects response. They then gave the new version to another class and taped the discussion.

Perhaps the most important use of the computer is as a means of recording and sharing responses to texts. Thus, presenting literature and recording responses become parts of the same package.

The computer is an excellent means of storing information that can be retrieved at a later time by the writer or by somebody else. It is, in this respect, a word processor and a card catalogue.

It can add art too.

This use can play a major role in the lives of students as they read texts and record their understandings of them. A student enters an initial response in a notebook file. The student then adds a series of questions he or she wants answered and brings these to class and raises them with the group. Later, the student enters the answers and his or her responses to them. These lead to a major question for a paper. The student next goes to the library, locates a number of sources on the issue, and enters the quotes and the bibliographic information. With all of this, the student has a file that can be used for reference and inclusion in the draft. It can get bigger and bigger— just like the file for this book, which filled two discs.

There is an expansion of the individual notebook growing into a paper on the text. One student's response can be added to by another student who is linked to the first through a computer network. And then by a third and a fourth. These students do not have to be in the same school, thanks to electronic mail. The first student can then scan the later entries and revise the original note or add to it. This "conversation" can take place over time and distance.

The teacher can enter into this network with additional comments or questions.

Another class can also enter into the conversation.

The class does not have to be in the same city or state.

It does not even have to be in the same year.

From the compiled notebook can come a class composition. It can be reviewed and added to as subsequent readings and responses are entered. Then an editor can produce a final text. It could even be indexed and annotated. It could become a resource for other students who are writing papers. It could become an annotated bibliography.

Together with the text it can become a different form of the hypertext that next year's students can use to initiate their reading of the same text and thus add to the cycle.

The result is a "reading" of the text that transcends the individual, distance, and time. It can be seen as an historical record, a journal of understandings and perceptions upon the text, of commentaries upon commentaries. It can enable a variety of students to enter into a community of readers and responders. Without making too much of it, we think this could be a valuable resource for the literature class, particularly in that it can enable students "new" to a text to have some sense of how other students like them have read it—that these other articulations of response are viable and have merit, that the students are not alone in their doubts and uncertainties.

Of course, it could get out of hand. . . .

Information overload can result.

Like the other media, the computer can be used creatively to enable students to record and share their understandings of literature and to help them become members of the larger community of readers.

But What About Writing and All That Stuff You've Been Feeding Us All These Years?

Writing-about-literature or writing literature or writing LITERATURE? What about writing programs and free writing and expressive writing and writing from experience? How does "all that stuff you've been feeding us all these years" fit into a literature program? It hasn't, but it should. But . . . we hear some say . . . OK, "they" write poetry and stories but is it REALLY literature or LITERATURE? Our initial response to this is . . . "Does it really matter?" . . . . Are all writers "great writers" when they make their early attempts? Was Mozart, the accomplished "too many notes" composer, at five what he became by twenty-five? And yes, Joseph Conrad went to sea without his family's approval at the age of sixteen but didn't write his first story until the age of twenty-nine.

Are we expecting too much to have all secondary students write compelling fiction and nonfiction while they are still experience-gathering? What kind of writing can we legitimately expect from today's 12- to 17-year-olds? Is reading literature an appropriate experience to write about? What can we expect them to record in their responses to literature? How long does it take for a "sense of literature" to evolve?

We ask these questions *in response* to such requests as the following— typical we think of what is asked in literature anthologies for secondary-school students, tacked on to the end of a series of questions about the literature they have just finished reading:

"Find a collection of tall tales in the library. Write a paragraph summarizing one of these tales."

or

> "Write a paragraph in which you use several examples to show that animals are protected by their coloration . . . . Open your paragraph with a sentence that states the central idea. You may use this sentence if you like: 'Natural coloration helps animals conceal themselves from their enemies'."

And then there are the types of assignments that simply ask "what" and "why" and sometimes "how" after a reading. Well, we suppose teachers can make of these what they will, but why? What, really, is their purpose? Do novels and stories in anthologies have questions tacked on at the end? Do the kinds of questions found after the "reading" selections really take the reader any further than that reader might go without them?

Finally, one last group of questions before we try to suggest some answers to all of them. When we ask students to write in response to literature should we focus on the writing or, as much as possible, on the content of the response? How does this affect what and how we evaluate what students write in response to literature? What are we really after when we get them to write in response to literature? What can we expect when we ask a whole class to write in response to a common novel, or poem or play? What kinds of writing fulfill our differing purposes in the literature classroom?

What About Literature as a Form of Writing?

The "writingless" literature classroom wastes a tremendous opportunity to have students write about something other than themselves but, yet, still close to themselves. By experiencing characters and situations and language crafting that literature provides, writers have always had available to them sources for subjects or topics, perspectives on those subjects or topics, and inspirations for crafting in their own work that lead to new insights, new "statements," new perspectives still uniquely their own.

We read about writers who have ascribed the tremendous influence of one or other writers—for example, Conrad studied Flaubert and Maupassant closely, and both of them provided him with examples in his quest to "find the suitable form without smothering the idea being shaped and released" (Leo Gurko, *Joseph Conrad: Giant in Exile*, p. 31).

Lloyd Alexander claims that he has so many authors he relies on for models and inspiration that he forgets the names of half of them. He then goes on to name Shakespeare, Dickens, Twain, Lewis Carroll, and adds that there might be a dozen.

Yes, we are strongly suggesting that there exists between literature and writing a very close and natural link—a symbiotic relationship. All writers confess to having been strongly influenced by what others have written and, in turn, may similarly influence other writers in their immediate surroundings and, if their contributions survive, may also have an impact on writers 100 years hence. Students report that reading a new author can give them a new way of organizing their writing.

To explore the possibilities that literature offers to its readers through writing, let's consider once more why one might study literature at all and then link these reasons with writing activities that could potentially form the foundation not only for comprehension of, response to, and critical understanding of literary text, but also as a means of expressing oneself.

First, literature offers extended experience or vicarious experience of other lives, both imagined and actual. As to whether or not these can be labeled "real," we believe that "reality" is very much in the eye of the beholder. The streamers of red thread that sweep across a devastated planet long after a large-scale atomic war are as "real" as the red Ferrari driving down a street once we enter into the reality of Anne McCaffrey's novel *Dragonsong*.

Second, literature offers the opportunity for insight into human behavior and the hidden thoughts and emotions that few of us have the opportunity for seeing in "real life." In the latter, much of this is carefully masked for all kinds of reasons. In literature, writers present what they penetrate through their characters and allow us to explore the differences between surface behavior and the hidden self. By the time the child is an adolescent this process is well underway and much of the preoccupation of the adolescent is concerned with the self in relation to others and how others perceive that self. The mask is beginning to be adopted although the colors and forms it may take are not yet fully in place.

Third, literature provides us with examples of social insight by particularly sensitized people—writers—so that we extend our perspective of individuals in such a way that we can see them as social beings, products of complex social contexts. Men and women are only heroes in the context of certain social situations—for example, repression of one form or other, natural disasters, economic deprivation. Black-and-white morality is often presented as shades of gray through the backdrop of experience that heroes and heroines must endure and surmount. A 13-year-old loses trust in his alcoholic parents after years of emotional, physical, and psychological abuse so that even when the parents undergo treatment and are "cured," the youngster can never absolutely believe them again.

Fourth, literature offers an aesthetic experience and insight into the creative experience. By reflecting on how writers achieve the effects of experience (e.g., moods, senses, rhythms) we can foster awareness of the writer's craft and, in turn, extend that awareness to student writing. Adolescent writers are already intuitively crafters when they write. For example, it isn't uncommon to find such writers using extremely short sentences to achieve emphasis or a series of short phrases to create cumulative effect. Much of this is, however, intuitive, although it may also be imitative.

Although the essence of what writers say and how they say it is probably essentially unplanned (Robert Hayden observed, "As you continue writing and rewriting, you begin to see possibilities you hadn't seen before"), the process of the activity involves a conscious kind of decision making much like decisions made by a potter who decides to work some more on refining the original creation so that the clay form is shaped this way rather than that.

John Updike describes the activity as a search for what one is saying. It involves writing and rewriting, and student writers who engage in a process-based activity are already very aware of making conscious choices related to crafting and shaping in their own writing. Literature, therefore, can delight and please through the shaping and not just the content.

Back to Composition

In the past ten years or so, and certainly since the appearance of the first edition of this book, the teaching of writing has undergone a quiet revolution in elementary schools and colleges and this revolution has now extended its influence into the junior and senior high school. It is by no means established, yet more and more English teachers are adopting what has become known as the *process-approach* or writer's workshop as the basis for writing instruction in the secondary school. This shift to relating the activity of writing to the text that emerges is particularly beneficial for providing a great range of opportunities in which students can write like "real writers" do and, therefore, provides an automatically closer link between writing and the study of literature.

Among the tenets of this newer approach to writing instruction are the following features:

Writing is recursive, moving back and forth among planning, drafting, revising, and editing.

Writing is both private and public—at times we withdraw and at others we need company—i.e., we need to talk with other writers, we need feedback from other writers and readers.

Writing is an activity involving one or more drafts depending on what the writer wants to say and to whom. It is related to the intended audience, how the writer will "say" his or her piece, and the amount of time available.

Writers take responsibility for their writing and make decisions as to when a piece is "finished" and when it is not.

Writing involves stops and starts, dead-ends, alleyways, and the path is not always clear—the writer does not necessarily know exactly what it is he or she wants to say until there is opportunity to stand back and reflect on it.

Writing is, first, about ideas and experiences and the early phases of the activity must necessarily allow attention to be focused on those aspects rather than on the editing/proofreading phases which, for "real writers," occur at a time when they are ready for publication, either formally or informally.

We have briefly described the main understandings about writing that relate to the cognitive aspects of the activity. However, research shows that real writing has real readers, that real writing involves decision making in response to intrinsic motivation and to potential readers. Writing is a social activity with both an intrinsic purpose for writing and an audience of readers that helps determine the outcome.

Writing folders; conferences with peers as well as teachers and other adults; feedback related to content, purpose, and audience; the use of journals as writer's logs or notebooks (compendia for collecting ideas that may or may not be taken up at a later date); and a shift in both student and teacher attitudes toward revision as a process of working or crafting through the raw material of ideas and experiences—all of these are actions, behaviors, and attitudes that lend themselves very well to talking, exploring, and writing about literature.

More emphasis is also now placed on student writers choosing their own topics and believing that they have valid and valuable things to write about than was the case in the traditional writing classroom. But, as teachers are becoming aware of the value of connecting reading and writing, they are also implicitly acknowledging that ideas come from "somewhere," and in this respect writing as part of a literature program offers a potentially extraordinary range of "things" to write about either directly or indirectly. As we noted earlier, professional writers freely acknowledge the influence of other writers on them, and no one has yet claimed that this influence operates exclusively at the level of form. Freedom in topic choice is an acknowledgment that we write best when we write about what we know most. This knowledge, however, need not be exclusively based on firsthand experience. Indeed, if it were, how much could be told? Rather, we believe that the knowledge and experience we have is an amalgam of firsthand experience and perception combined with vicarious experience and perception. Literature, again, offers a tremendously rich and diverse set of experiences.

So What Shall They Write?

If writing about literature is integrated with an activity-based approach to writing, students need not always write in response to the same piece of literature, nor need they always write in response to the same assignment provided by the teacher. Either of these approaches can result in a kind of deadliness that kills both interest in literature and the natural capacity to know one's own response. Look for a moment at the following essays composed by two ninth graders when asked to write a letter of advice to an incoming freshman about how to do well in literature:

> Hi Dan,
>
> Thanks for your letter. So you're getting nervous about 9th grade literature classes. Well, don't worry about a thing. Ninth grade is easier than it seems. There are only a few things that you will need to know. First of all, know how to spell and study your spelling vocabulary every week. Every time you have a final, 1/2 of it is vocabulary words. Next, always read the book you're assigned because the test you have over them will be very specific. Also remember never to use bad grammar in class. The teachers will get on your back for that. That's basically it. I hope that you do as well as I did.
>
> Good luck in 9th grade.

The second letter is less deadly—the writer knows how to work the system somewhat more confidently—but as with the first writer, it tells us how not to have students respond to literature.

> Dear Little Person—
> Who-is-one-year-younger-than-me,
>
> English is really a fun class, but you have to have 5 things to be able to succeed in class. Here they are:
>
> (1) Come well dressed, (2) Have a black pen, (3) Have enough money to be able to . . . OOPS! . . . Wrong list! (Just kidding)
>
> 1) Do your vocabulary—every week you get 10 words w/sentences to write. DO THIS because otherwise, you will probably sink.
>
> 2) Be nice—the teacher will probably think that you're a head, neo-nazi, prep, stuck-up, snot, etc. and automatically give you the appropriate grade.
>
> 3) Don't do other homework in class (or read, too). I know someone who does that (he sits right next to me), and I don't think he's all that, for lack of a better word, "Here."
>
> 4) Do know the names of the authors of the books and stories—these will ALWAYS be test questions.

5) Enjoy yourself—everything seems stupid to you if you don't want to learn something, but the literature is diverse enough for anybody to enjoy as long as you let go of the "I have to please. . ." idea, which is completely stupid, anyway.

Follow this list and enjoy your life in 9th grade.

Good luck.

Writing That Is Directly Related to Literature

Response Writing

Writing in any extended form immediately requires a mental engagement with literature that can be avoided in spoken response. This is so because extended writing seems to require us to organize our thoughts in some way and also requires us to think beyond the obvious. Extended writing draws out of the mind of the reader more information, more reflection, more wrestling than, for example, either group discussion or brief responses to questions will do. In part, this is a result of not having the question as a prop and as a means of providing only the essential information. A good assignment eggs us on to say more on our own initiative, if only because the page has to be filled. Writing seems to have a spin-off effect—a sentence generates another sentence until we have provided a composite view of what we think and feel. In contrast, questions requiring short answers (e.g., "Who was the main character in *A Catcher in the Rye*?") automatically set up barriers to further growth.

We could liken extended writing in response to literature to taking a journey either with no intention of following any given path (often the impressionistic, personal response) or taking a guided tour of the terrain to be covered (more likely an analytic response). In either case, a journey implies that some distance will be traveled, the traveler and the terrain determine the stopping points, the dallying and rendezvous locations may be modified as the journey progresses and, ultimately, when the journey is over, the traveler has a substantial experience to record and ponder over.

Another powerful argument in favor of extended written responses relates to the nature of writing itself. We know that when we first explore the extent of our knowledge and perspective on a topic we often discover both what we do and don't want to say about it. Additionally, the early forays into writing about a topic help us to discover both what we do know and don't know and to send us scurrying back to find out more if need be.

We now understand what real writers have always understood: that the early phases of writing about something enable us to "clear the mental decks"—get rid of intrusive material and unburden our memory capacity. Writing itself is a juggling act requiring us to balance attention-giving to content, structure, style, and perspective as well as the ubiquitous domain of spelling and usage. The less we need to juggle in competition with other matters requiring attention, the more likely it will be that we can come up with uncluttered insights into whatever it is we write about.

In asking students to write, we ask them to reformulate experiences for themselves and to transform them into a form capable of being understood and appreciated by others. Furthermore, writing about literature (particularly in the analytic response mode) requires the ability to generalize, to evaluate, and to synthesize. These critical thinking skills also develop classificatory skills, especially those related to determining relevance and the ability of relating part to whole and whole to part as students discuss in extended form how plot illustrates the theme or a line in a poem relates to another one in a different stanza, both illustrative of what appears to be the writer's or poet's intention.

In conclusion, literature offers a more immediately accessible content to write about than, say, history, biology, or economics. The experiences portrayed in literature are related to all human experience, however remote, but more importantly, the responses of the characters to those experiences have a common touchstone in all of us simply because we are human too. So, if a character is jealous, disillusioned, sad, delighted, ingenuous, or scheming, these are recognizable human traits and, as such, provide us with the opportunity of engaging directly at least at this level of the work. In this respect, literature is a natural platform from which we might dive in order to explore how others negotiate life's currents. And the text itself is there as a total experience, available to refer to again and again.

Exploring Literary Response Through Writing

Writing in response to literature, whether formally or informally, can include a wide range of activity, from brainstorming, early draft forms, impromptu or spontaneous writing, to "publishable" writing (the "finished" product). In fact, it covers the full range of raw to finished writing. Not every piece of writing should be graded; not every piece should be "finished," not every piece needs to be read by the teacher or by other students. Writing that may be felt by the student to have potential for development could be filed in a writing folder.

At times, a student may not even want to write something in response to a reading, and we suggest that this, too, should be an acceptable alternative. How many times have we put down a book, just having finished it in the pre-dawn hours, and wanted nothing more than to be allowed to let it soak through? If we want to encourage our students to be *readers* of literature we have to let them behave like real readers do (at times, if not always). Yes, our agenda for moving them on to various overt acts of engagement with a reading is there, and as teachers we have a responsibility for helping students become more sensitized readers. Are we arguing that letting a book soak in is a response? Yes, we are. And for those who fear that we won't know if a student is really doing so and is merely goofing off, we'd suggest that closer observation of behaviors should put those fears into perspective. We've all been in classrooms, teacher-led and "proof-of-response dominated," in which visible signs of "paying attention" belie the reality of student "switch-off." The half-awake pose, the doodling, and the wandering through the rest of the work with a finger on (we hope) the right page is more common than not. That's not the same as reading intently and then staring into space.

How to entice students to become really interested in the literature we ask them to explore is always a vexing question for most teachers. Allowing them to behave like adult readers is one way of doing this. Have the students keep a notebook and encourage them to record passages, extracts, entire poems, etc., that intrigue them, delight them, or catch their attention in some way. Encourage them to jot down what literary figures have said or written about their writing to provide them with their own records of these insights into the creative act. Collections of letters, biographies, autobiographies, literary essays, and interviews with writers are rich sources for these kinds of records.

We're not proposing recipes for writing about literature, but we can suggest some ways of grouping the kinds of writing that students might do to help us keep track of what they have attempted and what they have steered away from over a period of time. You will notice that within these suggested groupings (what we have called "Functions of Writing in Response to Literature") we can have students write impressionistic self-examining responses (i.e., what the work does to them) and also analytic text-examining responses (what they think *about* the work itself). None of the groupings we have suggested anywhere in this chapter are mutually exclusive and none fits neatly into a clean slot all of its own. Ultimately, the teacher and the students determine the types of writing done.

Functions of Writing in Response to Literature
Writing to Learn—
  e.g., responses in journals, logs.
  Character profiles
  Characters from other characters' perspectives
  Alternative, hypothetical endings
  Summary
  Reviews
    Criticism
    Evaluation

Writing to Convey Emotions:

    Letters to friends about books read

    Journals, diaries

    Students select form best suited to
        express written response at the
        emotional level to a novel, story or
        a poem (e.g., a poem, a reflective
        piece, an "episode" or "scenario").

Writing to Imagine:

    Creative spin-offs—not necessarily
        related to the literary text/s being
        dealt with but possibly exploring the genre and mode.

Writing to Inform:

    Open-ended questions for exploring student
        understanding of literary texts

    Analysis of literary aspects of the work

    Critical appreciation through writing

Writing to Convince:

    Critical arguments

    Discussions about who should
        and should not be censored

    Book Reviews

Presenting something as complex as writing in any one- or, at best, two-dimensional way, doesn't really capture just how many simultaneous aspects are involved in any one writing act. For example, we've tried to illustrate some of the main functions we see that writing in response to literature may have. At the same time, we've said that we can ask students to explore responses to literature either impressionistically or analytically. Yet, we have also said that none of the categorizations are mutually exclusive. For the purpose of clarifying these multiplicities of purposes and kinds of writing that may be employed in exploring our responses and understandings of literature, we've provided a diagrammatic representation intended to illustrate them. We don't want to present something that can be fixedly categorized. In explanation, we want to suggest that although we previously listed "letters to friends about books read" under the function of conveying emotions we could also have listed that same form under the "writing to learn" function.

All of these activities can be encompassed by a view of writing that permits evolution, process, and refinement, and allows for the validity of the spontaneous notation or record. A literature notebook or folder much like the writing folder could be kept as a record for evaluation of the students' understanding and response to literature.

Functions of Writing in Response to Literature

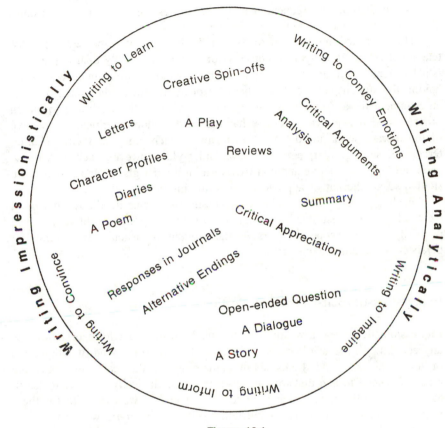

Figure 10.1

Elaborations

As we said earlier, response writing may either be impressionistic or analytic. If impressionistic, the focus will be less on the literary work itself but on the reader's subjective *reaction* to it. If analytic, the focus shifts from the reader's self to the literary work itself—that is, we write *about* the literary work rather than how we feel or think in reaction to it. Yet even the analytic response must contain seeds of the reader's impressionistic response, although in this instance the reader is actively attempting to understand the literary work itself.

The analytic or text-examining response might be termed an intellectual one in which the reader attempts to distance him or herself from the literary

work. We might also add, however, that not allowing adolescents the opportunity to articulate their impressionistic or self-examining responses to literary
works can hamper subsequent analytic responses, and we suggest strongly
that room be made for both.

How can writing be used to explore both types of response? Typically,
teachers have used analytic response writing more frequently than impressionistic response writing. The analytic written response frequently focuses on
having the student declare "the" thematic development of the work, or offer
an argument for and/or against an interpretive view of the work and so on. In
other words, the analytic response has the reader adopt a critical perspective
of the literary work and discuss it in terms of such things as theme, characterization, setting, plot, point of view, and style. However, such a response
need not be as restrictive and constrictive as it at first glance appears, and we
shall discuss alternative approaches later in this chapter.

Each type of response will be discussed in greater depth. At this point
we'd like to suggest that the *value* of written response to literature lies,
primarily, in the scope it offers to the student in articulating a range of
perspectives about the literary work.

Impressionistic Self-Examining Writing

Impressionistic response writing can be the loosest, freest form of writing in
any context. As the word "response" suggests, it is some kind of articulation
of how one feels and thinks about something (in this case, to something
read). We need to add that we can write impressionistically in order to learn,
to convey emotions, to imagine, or to inform just as we can write for these
purposes when the focus is on the text itself (i.e., analytic writing).

Therefore, the form of response writing can be whatever the individual
chooses and which best represents the nature of that response. For example,
some students may want to write a response to either prose or poetry in
poetic form because that form somehow allows them to express most closely
their thoughts and feelings. Others may choose to write a stream-of-
consciousness piece of prose with no discernible beginning, middle, or end
(structurally) other than the spatial top-to-bottom-of-page layout. Others may
want to write a more crafted piece—a creative, aesthetically based response.
Still others may want to write a journal entry—talking to the teacher or to
someone else about their thoughts and feelings. In the latter case, we'd
expect to see a conversational style, use of the first person, and a more
overtly subjective reaction full of statements such as, "I like it because. . . .
I didn't enjoy the way X did Y. . . ," and so on.

Another possibility is that students may wish to write a response that is
intertwined with interpretive thoughts, as in the following:

> The main concern or theme of the play *The Fire on the Snow* is somewhat hard to put into words but to me is summed up quite clearly in the author's Foreword to the play: It is, in its simplest terms, a struggle usually of man against man; in *The Fire on the Snow*: essentially of man against snow, the spirit of man against all that conspires to defeat him.

The writer of this particular piece, taken from an essay exploring the main issues in a play by Douglas Stewart (*The Fire on the Snow*, a drama about the last days of Scott and his companions after discovering that they had not beaten Amundsen to the South Pole), concludes:

> To me, the play *Fire on the Snow* is related to the themes I listed above, i.e., qualities of endurance, courage, humanness and determination all of which have a great bearing on the play. I enjoyed the play and think it was a great way of putting together such an historic event.

The student in this case was not academically oriented but demonstrates that remote as the experience responded to may be (a South Pole expedition in the early twentieth century) she had nevertheless developed both a close engagement with the text and an intellectual perspective of its power on the reader. Short-answer and multiple-choice questions don't offer the scope or the space for this kind of textual exploration.

One of the strongest arguments for encouraging students to write impressionistically, or expressively, about literature is that in doing so, they use their own *voice* and their own *language*. Writing about something not immediately one's own experience is challenging. Trying to do so in a style and from a perspective also not one's own is setting up a condition for frustration and potentially permanent alienation. We can look at impressionistic, expressive writing as a springboard for moving from the self to the work—the latter requiring, more often than not, use of language that is outside the regular experience of the adolescent (i.e., critical, analytical language).

We include here some examples taken from an activity during which eleventh graders were asked to write an essay expressing their thoughts on the content of Eudora Welty's short story "A Worn Path" and the meaning or significance of that content. The students were not given any prior information about the story but were provided with a brief biographical sketch of Eudora Welty. They were permitted to make notes during their reading of the story, including their reactions, confusions, associations, or anything else that occurred to them.

In this kind of open-ended writing experience, we find that many students do what we all do when writing about anything. The first articulations are usually forays into the forest, trying to discover what it is we really want to say, coming to grips with what we think something means, often halting attempts to define our own understanding. Such activity allows us to distance ourselves from what it is we think we know and want to say, thus enabling us to be more selective about what we want to write and how we express it. So with these students:

> *Student A:*
> The story "A Worn Path" is one with no standard plot or course of events. The main character, Phoenix Jackson, is an old woman who has to rely on the kindness of others to get what she needs. The supposed theme will be discussed below, as well as my ways of arriving at my conclusion.

> *Student B:*
> The theme of a "Worn Path" is patience. In this story, the granny walks to town to get a present and medicine for her grandson. She must of had much patience to walk the long journey.

> *Student C (as part of her conclusion):*
> It is also important to see how Phoenix thinks of the things that she sees on the way to town. She spoke to the animals and a thornbush that caught her dress like they were naughty children. She talks to herself when she crosses a creek on a log. Then, later on, when she rested, she thought she saw a young boy offering her some marble cake. When she goes through a corn field she calls it a maze. Her eyes often fooled her too. She saw a scarecrow and thought it was a ghost.

None of these examples would classify as literary criticism, but a major purpose of expressive response writing is, as we have suggested, to provide the opportunity for exploring what one understands and feels about a reading without the additional burden of having to put these thoughts and emotions into language that is formal and quite distant, often very unfamiliar to adolescents.

Analytic Response Writing

When we move to analysis, we move away from the impact a work has on us to examining the work itself and discovering what, in the work, causes it to have the effect it does. However, analytic writing does not mean that students have to become entangled by technical jargon. It also does not mean that exploratory writing and revision have to disappear. After the initial impressionistic responses recorded in language and forms familiar to the student, teachers and students may select from these those pieces that suggest further possibilities and which may be worked on for moving to a more objective discussion of the literary text. We could liken analytic response writing to moving from the private to the public domain. Now we describe for others the work as we perceive it and our reasons for doing so.

Because analytic writing assumes a shift to a more "critical" stance, using terms such as *theme, plot, rhyme, rhythm, figures of speech,* and so on are appropriate because we assume an audience that is familiar with the rhetorical styles of critical writing. Using such terms allows us to highlight certain aspects of the literary text that may be significant to our reading of it. However, the use of those terms themselves should not be our primary objective in having our students write analytically about the literary text. For example, the following essay illustrates not only a student's understanding of the role of Iago in Shakespeare's *Othello* but also the difficulty many students have in using language appropriate for formal critical writing:

> Shakespeare has written the play "Othello" as a tragedy, but included a mixture of love, justice and jealousy in writing such a play. Othello, so said by many, is the main character of the play because he is the tragic figure. He leads, and for this he is the tragic hero. However, in the sense of love, justice, and jealousy, Iago plays the main character of the play. Iago forces events to occur the way they do, and is almost totally responsible for the evil set loose in the play.

The student was obviously struggling to understand how it is that a main character (Othello) is not in fact a main character in terms of overtly directing the action of the play. It's not quite clear that professional literary critics themselves agree about who is the main guiding force of the action in this play so we can hardly expect a 16-year-old to give a definitive interpretation one way or the other! The students in this writing assignment were given the opportunity for revision and for conferencing with their English teacher, but opportunity had not been given for early writing of the expressive kind described previously in this chapter. Perhaps such writing may have helped this student and the others in the class to sort out the thematic and relational complexities in this play at their own level prior to having to write about them in a formal critical manner.

From our "Functions of Writing in Response to Literature," analytic writing can be seen as having at least three primary functions: writing to learn, writing to inform, and writing to convince. Neither of these functions is mutually exclusive. For example, a student may be asked to write a critical appreciation of a literary work. On the one hand this is an act of learning how to generalize (e.g., talking about the thematic development in the work) and linking whole to parts (e.g., selecting appropriate examples from the text in support of arguing a particular thematic development).

Additionally, the student may be asked to adopt a stance concerning an interpretation of the text (e.g., that the work is or is not reflective of an author's philosophical perspective on life), which requires the student to develop an argument and, hence, a position as well and defend it. In engaging the student so deeply in the text, through adopting a position about it, we can assume that (1) the student has read the text quite closely, (2) has remembered most of it and been able to translate it into his or her own understanding and experience, (3) has already exercised some degree of interpretation about the text, (4) has analyzed it into categorical parts (e.g., plot, theme, episodes, characters who are most and least important), (5) has synthesized it (been able to relate parts to whole and see parts in relation to each other), and (6) evaluated it (drawn some kind of judgment about the text).

Thus, in writing a critical appreciation, we can argue that students learn a great deal about the text, about their own response to it, and about the responses others may have had, and they demonstrate that learning to us (i.e., writing to learn, to inform, and to convince).

To clarify the arguments we have made here, we have included an essay written by a tenth grader on George Orwell's *Animal Farm*. Students were asked to argue the position linked with the following question:

> "*Animal Farm* is a story for children about talking animals. Do you agree? Discuss the reasons for your decision."

Of course it's a loaded question, because as a teacher of literature we know the novel is a satire (at least we believe it is) and therefore the astute student of literature should argue that it is much more than a story about talking animals. The third and final draft of the essay is reproduced here.

> George Orwell tells us, in *Animal Farm*, of a story about a rebellion by animals over the farm owner, Mr. Jones, who was an oppressor. The story is one of a seemingly victorious rebellion, which is represented by a group of talking animals. However, because the book is not as we would normally expect to find one of this kind—that is, without a leader in history whom we can refer to, and place a name to, we must not, and can not refer to *Animal Farm* as a children's book or one solely for children.
>
> In writing *Animal Farm*, George Orwell has given us almost two books within the one story; a book on two different levels. One in a superficial way. The other requiring us to interpret the words in greater depth, and relate them to the main theme of the book—Power. This "power" theme is also to show how power causes eventual corruption of an "ideal" society (without class distinction). However, "almost" is an important word, as Orwell's fine line between portraying a message to man, and telling a children's story leans more toward the former, than the latter.
>
> Although Orwell states at the beginning of the book *Animal Farm—A Fairy Story*, we should not read the book thinking that the story is merely for the amusement of a reader who wishes to find out about animals who tend to themselves on a farm. Instead, we should be able to sense something more in the book, even though he welcomes us to the story with the above statement. Some examples of this are: the event of the Rebellion; the partaking of human voices, and, a specific example is the ordering of death after "trials" for crimes which were never actually committed (p.

74). These suggest that there is more than a "story about talking animals" because they are taking on many human traits.

However, other factors may attribute to the belief of the book being a children's story. One example of this is the cover of the book—the title *Animal Farm* appears to be childlike, and, with the cover showing a small pig, one would not imagine that such a simple and plain exterior could contain such an important and interesting experience that Orwell expresses within the bindings of *Animal Farm*. The book, too, as in children's stories, is not long, and on reading it, we find the writing and language are simple, as well as containing a simple plot—all these add up to a children's story.

Yet Orwell's book also shows many traits throughout the story, which point toward the fact that this novel is related greatly to humans, their lifestyles, and his theme and theory of power. In fact, the whole story has animals performing tasks that humans alone can normally accomplish and that animals would be unable to do. This is the case in Napoleon's making of deals for the sale of wood. His cunning ways bring a high price for the wood, and Napoleon is once again thought of as being wise, great and fair to all.

We are shown here, that not only do the animals take on voices, but they also display many human faults. At this time in the story, when the pigs and Napoleon seek and keep on striving for greater power, the condition and health of the overworked "laborers" not only declines, but so does the state of Animal Farm. Thus, Orwell is reinforcing his views on power, and how it can break down an equal society into classes such as in *Animal Farm*. His point being to show us that an equal society is a dream and not an achievable reality. Here we can also see Orwell's purpose for writing the book showing through his experiences of war time and fighting for a society without classes, is difficult and even impossible.

We can therefore see that his story carries more than a book holding a fable about talking animals, and remembering that children's fairy stories are concluded with "the underdog" and "the good guy" coming out as victors, after violence and terrorism (as in *Animal Farm* to portray the struggle for the maintenance of power; natural leadership and human nature) we have even further evidence that *Animal Farm* is not a book written entirely for children. This is because the inhabitants of Animal Farm ("the underdogs") are still not happy with their situation. They are once again under an oppressor (Napoleon, the pig) and are once again, divided into groups of authority, and class distinction, as they were before the Rebellion.

Three drafts were written of this essay and the class as a whole enjoyed pre-writing discussion about the issue raised in the essay. A period of five weeks was allowed for the final draft to be submitted, and conferences were held with students after each of the two drafts were submitted for review. Students determined the final draft as being their best effort at this time.

Writing about literature in this way is demanding and requires that students grapple with abstractions that may be outside the common experience of adolescents. Consequently, we can expect that students in this age group and, we think up to the end of high school, finding essays of this kind very challenging. First, they need to be able to know the function of the specific mode—satire—then they need to be able to select appropriate and telling examples from the work to support any argument they put forth. Second, they need to be able to argue—that is, the rhetorical mode they are asked to write in—which, in itself, is a hypothetical stance requiring some persuasive abilities to convince the reader. Third, they do know about power, in both the concrete form—parent-child struggles, school bully, teacher vs. student tugs of war—and in the abstract form as a social and political concept. This requires an imaginative and cognitive leap from its workings in a literary context to the general and, perhaps, to illustrations in the world around them.

Given these challenges, we feel the writer of the essay illustrated here has demonstrated the value of writing in this way (despite some infelicities of organization and expression) for several reasons. First, it moves the writer from the concrete to the abstract and, hence, develops analogical reasoning skills. Second, it requires the writer to focus on text rather than on self and, therefore, helps the student develop an objective stance that paves the way for critical appreciation of the qualities of literature even though they may not personally *like* the subject or the manner in which the author has, for example, concluded a story. Third, it helps students develop generalizing and reasoning skills that, at later stages, enable them to link together other books and issues and, therefore, broadens the scope of literary appreciation. Of course, these are long-term effects, but the process of becoming a critically appreciative reader of literature is a long-term one and certainly not brought about by short-answer questions that limit the scope of thought and argument.

Any extended writing activity that requires students to stand outside their personal response to the literary text can have similar effects. We should remember, though, that the kinds of skills we're asking for in this kind of writing are, essentially, adult ones and we consequently need to modify our expectations. We're just not going to get a professorial version of a critical essay of the kind represented in this chapter from 14- to 16-year-olds (and do we really want one?), but we can help them extend their experience of literary text from personal to more public through writing experiences of the analytic kind.

Literature Written by Students

One of the functions of writing combined with literature is, as we suggested, writing to imagine—that is, writing literature. Despite the concerns many teachers have about students not being able to define such terms as metaphor, oxymoron, hyperbole, rhyme, rhythm, and so on, students, when they write literature themselves, demonstrate remarkable skill in using language illustrative of these "devices." Writing literature can, therefore, offer wonderful opportunities for exploring the special manipulation of language that this mode often utilizes.

An example of a controlled use of rhyme and meter to maintain a humorous, light-hearted style is demonstrated in the following poem by an eighth grader:

MY DOG, MY CAT, MY HAMSTER AND ME

My dog, my cat, my hamster, and me
Sleep together so peacefully.
My cat on my pillow, close to my head;
My dog on the floor in his little dog bed.
I roll over which makes my cat hiss,
And my hamster stops spinning his wheel
long enough to watch this.

Sometimes I wish I had no pets to lie
by my head or to growl from the floor.
If I had no dog to sit and whine at my door?
Or if I had no cat to hiss or to scratch up my face,
And no hamster to spin and keep me wide awake?

So really I'm glad for my hamster, dog and cat,
Even if they don't really know that.

The poets John Ciardi or Shel Silverstein would probably be proud of that young writer! Or there is this poem (by another eighth grader) perfectly capturing the epitaph style but with the quality of the limerick:

GRAVESTONES BY HENRY BONES

Here lies Danny Lee,
He almost learned,
to water ski.

Here lies John Marks,
Now buddies
With the sharks.

Here lies Brian Sute,
He almost learned
To parachute.

Here lies Peter Nunn,
Was foolin' around
With a gun.

Here lies Henry Bones,
Died engraving,
Funny tombstones.

And the control, the sensitivity to the special power of language we mainly see in literature, is also visible in prose.

> *Gladiator*
>   Circling the ring, I contemplated my next move. Right now he was ahead, but I knew he wouldn't be for long. He was weak, scared, no fire in his eyes. I decided on an all-out attack. With all my might I thrust my shoulder into his gut. Without thinking, I wrapped my arms around his legs. This was it—everything or nothing. My body flexed. In an all-out show of power I heaved him to the floor. He had lost his will to live. I wrapped my arms around his head, wishing only to end the battle mercifully. A hand slapped on the mat. Time rushed before me. I was not a gladiator fighting for my life. I was back on the school Wrestling Squad.

Writing literature can provide students with motivation for revision (often perceived by novices and professionals alike as an onerous chore) if we provide them with opportunities to apply their aesthetic responses to literature they read to their own crafting of literature. Leaving the writing of poetry at the level of expressive, impressionistic response does not do this. And there will always be poems and stories that will never leave the personal journal. But some of our discussions with eighth graders about writing from the perspective of other writers resulted in a better understanding of why writers revise and, according to their teachers, in a greater enthusiasm for revising even their creative products. In our discussions, students showed tremendous interest by asking additional self-initiated questions about what writers say of their own writing, as witnessed by statements such as the following:

> Very few people that I know of, and I believe that this includes the greatest writers who have ever lived, ever got it right the first time. And I think the secret is, as you know and every writer knows, the hardest part is not writing but rewriting. That is where the work truly begins, and once you've caught onto that you will have understood a great deal.
>   (Lloyd Alexander, interview in *Language Arts*, 61(4) April 1984, pp. 411–413)

Students really related to statements like the following, as could be seen in nods of the head, heads suddenly lifting upward in surprise and the look of "that's me" on their faces:

Writing to me is a voyage, an odyssey, a discovery because I'm never certain of precisely what I will find. (Gabriel Fielding)

As you continue writing and rewriting, you begin to see possibilities you hadn't seen before. (Robert Hayden)

How do I know what I think until I see what I say? (E. M. Forster)

More often I come to an understanding of what I am writing about as I write it. (Frank Conroy)

From Donald Murray, *Learning by Teaching: Selected Articles on Writing and Teaching*, pp. 85–86.

Writing literature, possibly more than writing informational, transactional prose mainly required to demonstrate understanding of a literary text, offers students the opportunity to gain an appreciation of the crafting nature of aesthetic writing. But more than any other form of writing commonly practiced in school, it offers the opportunity for writers to develop their own style, to strengthen their own voice.

We offer a cautionary conclusion, however. Not all students will be comfortable with literary creative writing, nor should we assume that they ought to be. This domain of writing is closest to what we might call "innate talent"—some will be naturally more inclined toward it than others, just as some are more naturally inclined to scuba diving than others. In the school setting, therefore, this kind of writing ought not be used for formal evaluation or grading since we see it operating more as a function of individual preference. For here we face, full on, the essential elusiveness of the literary text, no matter how hard we attempt to analyze it. And who can, with confidence, say of any literary text that "this way is better than that"?

Concluding Thoughts

We've offered some of the ways in which writing and literature can be meaningfully related in the English classroom. The sensitive English teacher will, without doubt, find other ways. As with other writing done in the English classroom, we would like to suggest several maxims to promote ways in which the experience can be rewarding, enjoyable, and challenging:

Do allow for choice in form as well as topic.

Do allow for opportunities to *not* write in response to readings.

Don't expect students to write a response for every reading.

Do provide for varied writing experiences to encourage variations in how we interpret a literary work.

Do respond to student writing as one responds to established authors.
Do not always have a grade for every written piece.
Do encourage students to "publish" their own literary works.
Provide opportunities for nongraded literary creative writing.
Provide opportunities for impressionistic response.

Writing is an activity with an end in view.
X. X

A Note on Giving Assignments and Feedback

In the last chapter we had a good deal to say about writing in all its various forms. In this interchapter we want to add a special note on the more formal aspects of writing, those times when we give assignments and then provide feedback. A lot of the writing that students will do will come from these assignments. The writing will also be their journals, their topics, but sometimes we give them assignments in part because the system demands it, and in part because we want to help them do well in other writing situations. Students will have to take writing tests, final examinations. They will have to write on demand. It's wrong not to help them succeed. Two ways we know of are to make clear to them how to analyze the assignment and how to use feedback.

Making and Analyzing Assignments

Too often we will simply give the students a topic rather than plan out the nature of the writing task we want them to perform. Yet the setting of the task can either provide a stimulating activity for our students or it can be thoroughly confusing and stultifying.

Seeing the Nature of the Problem

A writing task may be thought of as providing a cognitive problem for the writer, and it may also be thought of as offering the writer a discourse function to be met. In the array of cognitive problems, the writer may see himself or herself as alternatively transcribing material where the form and the content are given or available in long-term memory (reading or lecture notes, certain lists, stream-of-consciousness journals); organizing or reorganizing material that is known or available (writing reports, directions, narratives, and the like); or inventing or generating new material into new structures.

The discourse functions that may underlie a writing task are the metalingual, where the discourse is primarily to help the writer learn; the expressive or emotive, where the writer is seeking to release opinions or feelings; the referential, where the writer is aiming at presenting information clearly; the conative, where the writer is seeking to convince or persuade the reader; the poetic, where the writer is focusing on the text as an object to delight or please the reader; and the phatic, where the aim is to keep writer and reader in touch.

The first thing for the student to figure out is what is the cognitive task. *Write an essay in which you compare* Death of a Salesman *to other tragedies you have read this semester. Is it a tragedy?*

What is the function? to inform.

What is the cognitive demand? to fit the example into a category. Not much invention, mostly plugging into the definition.

But the assignment of a composition consists of more than cognitive demand and discourse function. We can identify fifteen dimensions of a composition assignment:

A. Instruction	**I.** Tone, Style
B. Stimulus	**J.** Advance preparation
C. Cognitive demand	**K.** Length
D. Purpose	**L.** Format
E. Role	**M.** Time
F. Audience	**N.** Draft
G. Content	**O.** Criteria
H. Rhetorical specification	

The actual assignment you give must be scrutinized to ensure that it is doing what you want. One way to handle this is to make out a task specification sheet for each composition assignment, particularly those used in assessments that are meant to be comparable, such as semiannual placement or exit examinations.

You have the students do this too:

Write an essay of about four pages in which you compare Death of a Salesman *to other tragedies you have read this semester. Is it a tragedy? You should write for a student who has read the plays but has not been to class so as to explain the nature of tragedy and how* Death of a Salesman *fits. You should plan to spend one period drafting your paper and then a second period preparing a final copy. Your essay will be scored for its clarity, organization, and use of examples.*

What's the cognitive demand? to organize known information.

What's the function? inform.

Any restrictions on:

   Role: classmate of reader

   Tone: formal

   Content: limit to tragedies read

   Rhetorical specification: essay

   Format: no

   Length: four pages

   Time: two periods

   Audience: student

Advance preparation: no.

Draft or final: final.

Criteria: content, examples, organization.

With this sort of analysis, a student can better work through the assignment and not make any dumb mistakes. It works for those external examinations too.

What Sort of Feedback to Give to a Composition

One of the problems that faces teachers is that of having to deal with the mountain of compositions that students hand in. It is easy enough to ask the students to write something, but then you have to look at each composition and make some judgment as to its quality and how it might be improved.

This problem has been the object of considerable research, which leads to some recommendations that can help ease the burden of the load of unmarked papers.

1. It is not necessary to give detailed comments on every composition. It is better to save the lengthy comments for those compositions that the students have a chance to revise or rewrite.

2. It is best to give feedback as quickly as possible. Having to wait two or three weeks causes students to lose interest in their writing.
3. It is always good to have some positive comment on each composition. The returned composition should not consist only of the original with corrections and negative comments.
4. Whenever it is possible, a good way of giving feedback is in a conference or small-group discussion when the teacher and student can go over the composition together.
5. At various times during instruction it is good to have the students provide the feedback to each others' writing. They get practice in judging compositions; they often learn how to improve their own compositions; and they usually give good suggestions for improvement.
6. Whenever you mark or comment upon a composition, you should not focus on only one aspect such as spelling or grammar. These are the aspects of writing that make it readable, but they do not make it meaningful. The ability to produce effective discourse is judged when teachers comment on the quality and scope of the content of the composition, on the organization of the composition, on the style and tone of the composition, and on the personal impression the writing made on the reader.

When you mark compositions it is useful to keep students' success in writing a legible text separate from their success in creating meaningful discourse. One way of doing this is to prepare a brief form that can be attached to each composition. One version of the form might look like this:

	Poor				Excellent
Discourse-Level Qualities					
Quality and Development of Ideas	1	2	3	4	5
Organization and Structure	1	2	3	4	5
Style and Tone	1	2	3	4	5
Text-Level Qualities					
Grammar and Wording	1	2	3	4	5
Spelling and Punctuation	1	2	3	4	5
Handwriting and Neatness	1	2	3	4	5
My personal reaction	1	2	3	4	5
Comments:					

One virtue of this kind of scoring sheet is that it helps you to be sure that you are not letting one aspect of the composition overwhelm your judgment of the whole composition. It may be that a student has very good ideas and has organized them well, but has used a tone inappropriate for what is intended. It may be that another composition is perfectly correct in every way but contains very juvenile and unconsidered ideas given the general level of the student or the class.

By separating out one's judgment and examining the various aspects of writing competence, teachers are able to give a balanced perspective on their students' writing and prepare them for the varied sorts of judgments that the students will receive later on in life. Teachers can use these categories for judging all kinds of writing tasks, from a brief friendly letter to a summary to a narrative, reflective essay, or argument. Certain of the aspects are more important in some types of writing than they are in others. An effective style and tone becomes important in an argument; clear organization is important to a description or a narrative; and well-thought-out ideas are most important in a reflective essay. But to say that only one is important is to make that aspect a matter of emphasis; it is not the only consideration.

If you are working with college-bound students, you can go beyond this general scheme and can suggest to your students that there are sets of norms that they will run into in college and in other subjects. We found thirteen normative characteristics of United States academic writing against which teachers judge compositions:

Content. This dimension concerns the subject matter of the composition and the way it reflects the writer's manipulation of ideas, objects, and events. There are seven subaspects of content, which we might argue can be seen as fulfilling successively stringent criteria for academic writing:

1. **Adequacy of information.** There must be sufficient information to fulfill the assignment, which is to say the content must match the limits set by the assignment.
2. **Richness of additional information.** There may be additional information drawn from the writer's other reading or experience in the area. That information, however, must be clearly made relevant to the main focus of the assignment. Digression is not permitted.
3. **Relationships drawn among items of information.** The various discrete predictions or subtopics must be shown to be related to each other according to an acceptable principle of grouping (see 9 below). There can be no outliers.
4. **Inferences made beyond the scope of information.** The text is not to be a catalogue of information, but there must be some inferences drawn from the various bits of data.

5. **Synthesis.** There should be a drawing together of the inferences into a generalization. Taking four and five together, a composition should have an optimum of three levels of abstraction, from specific to first-order inference to second-order generalization.

6. **Evaluation.** The paper should in most cases go beyond the reporting of data and should make a judgment, preferably on rational grounds, concerning the merits of the inferences and the generalization.

7. **Alternatives.** The composition should consider alternative explanations or generalizations and show why the one proposed is superior. The paper should give evidence of an open, but decisive, mind.

Organization. This dimension concerns the optimum structure for the composition as a whole text as well as the arrangement of its subunits. Although the organization can be modified according to the conventions of particular academic disciplines, they still have the following common characteristics.

8. **Framing.** The composition needs to have a detectable beginning, middle, and end. Although the generalization need not be at the opening, it should be close to it and should be recapitulated near the end. The actual opening may take a number of appropriate forms. The development or middle must be longer than both opening and closing and may follow one of a number of acceptable formats for grouping.

9. **Grouping.** The information and ideas should be combined rationally, using a temporal, spatial, or classificatory structure. These three can be modified to form different complex structures such as cause-effect, comparison/contrast, or hypothesis testing.

10. **Unity.** The writer has the obligation to indicate the relationship among the parts that have been grouped. The grouping structure should be signalled with the appropriate lexical items for the selected grouping, and these should be rather more present than absent.

Style/Tone. This dimension refers to the manner in which the composition is presented and particularly the degree to which the manner approximates the conventional use of language in academic discourse.

11. **Objectivity.** The writer should use impersonal and detached language. There are some exceptions to this standard, particularly in the more "modern" subgroups of the humanities, but impersonality and detachment are still standard in the sciences and social sciences.

12. **Tentativeness.** There should be an ample number of semantic hedges and qualifiers to indicate that the composition is not dogmatic but a part of the academic scholarly dialogue.

13. **Metalanguage.** The composition should use an adequate number of markers to connect the propositions and the paragraphs. The text should in this sense make it easy for the reader to see the intended connections among propositions.

This scheme specifies the implicit model for academic writing that teachers in the United States use when they read. We have found that it is particularly useful to share these criteria with student writers, so that they can see that there are certain cultural norms that American teachers in various fields may well apply to their compositions.

We are not claiming that these norms are universally valid or should necessarily be considered as eternally correct, but they are the norms that many writing teachers will use to judge student writing, whether those students be native or non-native speakers, members of ethnic majorities or minorities.

Teachers who have used these marking criteria and have discussed them with their students have found that the students appreciate an honest discussion of what is being looked for in their writing. Some teachers have given forms such as the one shown above to their students for use in peer evaluation. This has been a particularly effective strategy, for it forces the student raters to look at many aspects of their colleagues' compositions.

Clear and honest feedback improves student performance in writing. Together with good assignments and time for planning, clear and consistent feedback that attends to both the text-producing competence and the discourse-producing comments of the student helps more students—especially minority students—write better. It also helps make for more accurate and consistent assessment of both entering and completing students.

CHAPTER 11

How Can a Poor Little Literature Program Survive in That Great Big World of Tests?

Nearly all that we have been saying in the earlier chapters of this book might as well go unsaid unless something is done about the world of tests that surrounds our students and our schools. The United States has been called test mad, and our major testing organizations are happily trying to encourage other countries to join them. Children are tested before they enter kindergarten, and they are subjected to standardized tests that are used to place them, channel them, label them, raise or lower the property values on their parents' homes, reward or punish their teachers and principals, and cause headlines in the local papers. Testing is a big industry, and those who reap the greatest profit are the test publishers and the real estate agents who can add $20,000 to the value of a property if it is in the "right" school district, which is the one with the highest test scores.

These tests generally do little good in helping teachers do their job better, and they do little to help students learn something more about school subjects except to suggest that certain students may need more help to make it over the hurdles. The result of most of the tests is to label students as "remedial" or "slow" or "gifted," and each label can be used to isolate the students rather than to help them work from their strengths or shore up their weaknesses.

A particular problem with these tests is what they do to the teaching of literature. They tend to kill off everything that we suggest should be nurtured. They do so not because the testing companies are malicious or evil but because the companies simply fill a perceived need—just like drug dealers.

Tests Measure What Our Students Are Learning and Tell Them What to Learn

Three decades of research in literature teaching and testing lead to a fairly simple summation:

1. Students generally learn what they are taught and don't learn what they aren't taught.
2. What students are taught is not always what teachers think is being taught.

Let us elaborate on these two points. When students are taught a concept or an approach to a text, by and large they demonstrate that they have learned what has been taught and exhibit it in a test situation. Conversely, if they have not been taught a particular text type or a particular way of looking at texts, and those are on a test, they won't get it right. They do not appear to have picked it up naturally.

American students demonstrate that they have mastered the lesson of being efficient readers who come up with the single symbolic and moralistic reading of a text much as if every poem had the characteristic of a fable or the pseudo-texts of the basal reader. This approach to the text is peculiarly American, and can be contrasted to the historical and intertextual approach of the Belgian or Italian student, the more stylistic approach of the English or New Zealand student, or the more psychological and evaluative approach of the Swedish student. Each of these groups of students appears to have mastered the critical approach of the teachers. That they move from a less consistent version of the approach to a more consistent version represents, we would argue, not growth but the painful result of a moderately effective educational system that fails to make the rules of the game apparent to the students clearly enough and allows them to learn by trial and error.

Not Learning What Isn't Taught

In addition to showing that students learn what they are taught, studies also demonstrate that they do not learn what they are not taught. Analysis of the patterns of performance on particular items and passages revealed that American students aged fourteen had greater difficulty both with the text that was more allusive and metaphorical than the literal narratives, and with items that dealt with issues of style and that called for knowledge of literary terms. They also had difficulty writing arguments. Such was not the case universally nor was it true of older students. An analysis of the textbooks and standardized testing programs in the United States shows that the main fare is relatively prosaic and the questions deal infrequently with literary terms or with writing arguments before the upper years of secondary school, if even then.

Lest anyone think that we are simply delivering old news, we should say that a recently completed survey of the tests of reading and literature used in secondary schools in this country indicates that little has changed. The texts are generally straightforward narratives with little figurative language, and the items deal with the efferent message of the text. There is an occasional item on style or structure, but these are insufficient to constitute a meaningful subscore. Most of the essay questions also deal with the description of a determinate meaning. Deconstruction, or reader response theory, has yet to find its way into the secondary school testing programs in the United States.

Learning the Wrong Thing

To establish the second of our two generalizations, we could simply point to the first and ask if the specifics that we have outlined match what is desired by the profession or preached by such groups as the California Literature Project or the College Entrance Examination Board. But we shall go a bit further. We studied the perceptions of students as to what constitutes a good student in literature. We asked students in the last years of high school to write a letter of advice to students about to attend their school on how to do well in literature classes. You saw two examples in Chapter 2, and content analysis of their responses reveals that a large segment of their advice deals with reading strategy—"sit in a hard chair," "take notes on what you are reading," "ask your mother what it means"; with writing strategy—"watch your spelling," "take a creative approach"; and with classroom politics—"find out the teacher's interpretation from the class the period before," "sit in the front row and ask questions." Very little advice deals with what we might think of as the substance of reading literature and writing out or discussing one's response to what is read. Literature classes are seen as reading for test taking and clearly not reading for exploration.

There has been a lot of talk in teachers' convocations about growth in English generally and in writing and literature study in particular. If there is growth in American students as they progress through the education system, that growth is not free or "natural," but is the result of a system of training and nurture including a great deal of pruning and the steady administration of manure—particularly in the examination system. We do not think that system is a deliberate "plot," but students have become moralizing symbol hunters not through some sort of natural Piagetian development from the general to the abstract and the familiar to the recondite, nor because literature teachers necessarily desire that outcome.

No, it is simply that such has been the nature of the questions hammered at students beginning in grade one, and promulgated by several generations of reading tests. The people who make up the reading tests aren't evil, Lord love them; they just don't know any better. The transition from "what is the main idea?" to "what is the symbolic significance?" is an easy one, and the fact that the main idea or a symbolic significance can be accommodated in a brief response to a multiple-choice question makes the whole matter of literature learning easy to teach, relatively easy to learn if only you catch onto the system, unenjoyable, and counter to what most serious thinkers believe about the nature of literature and its exploration.

Is there a way out of this situation? We think so. The main way is to redefine the domain of learning of school literature for these test makers in school districts, states, and publishing companies and make sure that the testing program covers the domain. It is simple. It is also very, very difficult. It requires convincing parents, school boards, testing companies, and textbook producers. Change the tests and you change the curriculum. It's as simple as that.

Changing the Tests by Rethinking the Domain

In order to change the tests, teachers and administrators cannot simply wish them away or attack them as evil. That approach has been tried and it has failed. Parents, students, and administrators have a right to know how well students are doing, and they even have a right to know how well they are doing in comparison with some standard. We do not think a comparison with an age group or a class is particularly meaningful. We would argue that it is better to see how students are doing with respect to a criterion, such as how well they have covered the subject. If we are going to attempt a reasonable alternative to standardized tests, we have to present a clear depiction of the domain and then develop a set of reasonable objectives and a rational means of showing the world the degree to which our students have met those objectives. To begin that task, let us look again at this domain of literature learning in school as we described it in Chapter 3. First of all, we can say that literature learning can be seen as a complex activity that involves not simply individual students, but students as a community, and that undertakes a set of acts and operations that define this activity as distinct from others such as "doing science," or "being historians," "cooking," or "driving."

Literature as a "Language Art"

The domain of school literature is usually seen as trying to squeeze into one of the language arts, which have often been defined in terms of reading, writing, speaking, and listening. Literature involves texts that people read or write, and when students read literature they often write about what they have read. Literature tests are simply a subtest of reading and maybe a topic for writing. It's just a different content from social studies.

As we said, we are uneasy with this definition. We become particularly uneasy when we look at the world of tests and see that literature is simply a vehicle for reading comprehension tests or for measures of writing skill or proficiency. To define the literature curriculum as simply a subset of reading and writing neglects a number of the acts that go on within the activity of literature education. We've mentioned a lot of them in this book.

Literature Learning as the Acquisition of Knowledge

Some people would define literature as a school subject that has its own body of knowledge. Recently, this body of knowledge has come to be called "cultural literacy." Narrowly defined, the body of knowledge refers to the names associated with a particular set of texts: authors, characters, plots, and themes. Even more narrowly defined it limits that body of knowledge to the texts from a particular cultural hegemony. We have suggested that this view is too limited. Literature as a body of knowledge must be expansive and must allow for the inclusion of a variety of cultures from around the world and particularly from a variety of groups within our own "melting pot," which keeps refusing to melt. It also must allow for the new, for change. Cultural literacy must include the new and must be ready to cleanse itself of the outmoded. Schools should include the past and the historical and should include many of the texts that students would not otherwise read. But they must not be too rigid about it.

The body of knowledge in literature could also be broadened to include critical terms like *metaphor, rhyme, plot,* and *irony,* as well as genres, schools or styles of writing, and entire critical approaches. Students should have acquired language about literature. They should also become aware of what the properties of novels, drama, and poems are thought to be, even though these definitions should not be too rigid. Poems do not always have to rhyme. Novels and stories can have minimal plots. The students should also become aware of some of such major critical theories as the mimetic theory of Aristotle or the expressive theory of Wordsworth.

Literature Learning as a Special Set of Preferred Acts

Throughout this book we have suggested that literary works are not read and talked about as other kinds of texts are read but are to be read differently. Louise Rosenblatt calls this kind of reading aesthetic and contrasts it to the efferent reading that one does with informational texts such as those of social studies and science. The current reading tests only measure efferent reading and by implication signal to students that it is the only kind of reading that is to be valued. As we suggested earlier in this chapter, a part of literature education involves the development of what one might call preferences, which is to say habits of mind in reading and writing. These preferences include particular approaches to reading and discussing a text. If we are to inculcate a preference for reading aesthetically, the examination system has to include measures of aesthetic reading.

In addition to ways of reading, literature education is supposed to develop something called "taste" or the love of "good literature," so that literature education goes beyond reading and writing and specific sets of preferences and habits of reading and writing. It includes the development of a tolerance for the variety of literature, of a willingness to acknowledge that many different kinds and styles of work can be thought of as literature, and an acceptance that just because we do not like a certain poem, this does not mean that it is not good. It can even lead students to distrust the meretricious or the shoddy use of sentiment. Experienced readers of literature can see that they are being tricked by a book or a film even when the trickery is going on.

A Model of the Domain of Literature Learning

The domain of school literature does not need to choose among these various views of literature teaching. In fact, as we discussed in Chapter 3 and will here elaborate, the domain is best viewed as divided into three interrelated aspects: knowledge, practice, and preference (see Table 11.1). The interrelationships are complex in that one uses knowledge in the various acts that constitute the practice and the preferences, and that the practices and preferences can have their influence on knowledge. At the same time one can separate them for the purposes of testing and curriculum planning.

To spend a few lines explaining Table 11.1, we would argue first that

TABLE 11.1. SCHOOL LITERATURE

Knowledge		Practice		Preferences	
Textual	*Extra-textual*	*Responding*	*Articulating*	*Aesthetic*	*Habits*
Specific text	History	Decoding	Recreating	Evaluating	Reading
Cultural allusion	Authors	Envisioning	Criticizing single works	Selecting	Criticizing
	Genres	Analyzing		Valuing	
	Styles	Personalizing	Generalizing across works		
	Critical terms	Interpreting			

school literature is different from literature outside of school, simply because schools are their own social and cultural institutions with their own rules. Students have to do some things together, and they have to respond to certain demands. School is its own life and school literature is like literature outside of school in that people read and bring their knowledge to bear upon what they read and display their preferences about their reading. But in school, students have to do these things more or less on demand, and they have to show their relationship to the group, the community of readers that is the class. They also have to do more writing and talking about their reading, and much of this is quite formal. They may have to engage in drama or filmmaking or other media work even when they are not quite in the mood to do so.

Interrelationships

The activity of literature learning appears to involve three closely interrelated and interdependent acts: knowledge, practice, and preference. The practices involve responding and articulating, reading and writing primarily, but they also might involve listening, viewing, speaking, and moving. For the sake of economy and to satisfy the test makers and users we will concentrate in this chapter on reading and writing. The practices are clearly informed and shaped by knowledge and they affect what is known in turn. We now know how heavily reading and writing rely on the use of knowledge in the head of the reader and writer: knowledge of words and their meanings, of syntax and grammar, of different kinds of organizations and arrangements like paragraphs and alphabetized lists, and of procedures and strategies for reading. The same applies to writing. In literature, there are certain special kinds of knowledge. Because literary texts often allude to other texts, they demand that readers know something of these texts. *West Side Story* makes its point because the reader knows something about *Romeo and Juliet*. Other works may make general allusions to personages from legend or folklore. These can be thought of as texts too, of course.

There is another kind of knowledge that marks the learning of literature and informs and is affected by the practice of reading. It includes knowledge of authors and what other texts they might have written as well as of when they might have lived and who influenced their writing. It also includes knowledge of literary terms and genres and conventions, such as the notation for act and scene divisions of a play or the form of a sonnet or the style that is known as realism or the term *dramatic irony*. It might even include knowing the strategies of a whole approach to reading and criticizing such as Freudian criticism or historical interpretation.

Some test programs include tests of this sort of knowledge all by itself, but we urge that such testing be minimal and only seen as an adjunct, albeit an important adjunct, to the testing of the practices of reading and writing, responding and articulating a response to literature. Reading literature as we have suggested throughout this volume is more than simply decoding or making out the plain sense meaning of the text. That is important, a necessary first step, but it should not be the be-all and end-all of a testing program—or a curriculum. Reading involves the creation or re-creation of the text in what has been called an "envisionment," a peopling of the text in the mind. This envisionment accepts the world of the text as another world that can be personalized and related to the reader's own world. It can be interpreted as having one or more possible meanings, and it can be analyzed both for its human elements and for its structure, tone, voice, and style.

In school literature, responding is accompanied by articulating, which is to say the production of some sort of formal statement about what has been read. Sometimes this writing is called *criticism*. People write about their understanding of what they have read and seek to make that understanding accessible to others. They seek to persuade other readers that their envisionment, personalization, analysis, or interpretation is not better than others but certainly acceptable and reasonable. Another form of writing may be to make some sort of general statement about the body of works that have been read, to draw connections between various texts. One could, for example, show what makes Langston Hughes's poems appear to be by the same author, or how Joseph Conrad's *Heart of Darkness* is like Dante's *Inferno*, or how Jane Eyre and Hester Prynne are sisters under the skin.

The use of knowledge in reading and writing has another dimension: the aesthetic, for when people read literature in school or out of it, they should engage in and with the text in such a way as to see it as a work of art to be experienced in and for itself. They can also judge the work and its effect on them. The judgment may be about its impact on them, about its form and structure, about its meaningfulness, or a combination of the three.

These sorts of judgments are to be encouraged in literature classrooms, as are the discussions that should emerge if, as is to be expected, a group of students disagree about the aesthetic merit of a particular poem or story. The aesthetic dimension of reading should be explored in writing and can be the focus of a part of the testing program. Certainly a set of tests could describe the aesthetic principles held by students and should also call upon them to justify their judgments. The aesthetic dimension of a literature program should also manifest itself in what the students select to read. The literature program should also show itself in the habits that students develop. The students at the end of a literature program such as the one we advocate should read a variety of different types of works and should not be turned away from literature, either classic or contemporary. In addition, they should have the habit of reading. And they should develop an eclectic approach to the various texts they read rather than become the moralizing symbol hunters we described at the beginning of this chapter.

That's a Nice Theoretical Statement. How Does It Work?

Evaluating the performance of your students in a response-centered curriculum—or any literature curriculum for that matter—means that you will have to find out what the students know, how well they read, how well they write about what they have read or are reading, and what is the nature of their aesthetic perceptions and judgments. That's no easy task. It might mean a battery of tests covering literary history, recitations or memorized literature, reading tests, writing tests, and measures of taste and preference. In the curriculum we are setting forth in this volume, however, the central focus is on the practice of responding and articulating, with due attention to the uses of knowledge and to the aesthetic dimensions of reading literary texts—that is, to judgments and preferences. The assessment package we would propose would feature students writing about what they have read and especially about what they are reading. There would also be records of class discussions, performances, and other sorts of expressions of response, from pictures to computer programs. For each student these papers and records could be assembled into a portfolio that would show to the world outside of the class that the students have learned something and are using their learning.

The Uses of Learning

We think Harry Broudy's idea of the "uses of learning" has particular relevance to the assessment and evaluation of learning in literature. Broudy sets forth four uses: replicative, applicative, interpretive, and associative. The replicative and applicative uses are those he finds to be most frequently addressed in schools. That is, people are to give back what they learn; they are to apply what they have learned directly to a new situation. In the case of literature, the replicative use of learning tends not to be directly assessed except in trivia contests and some quizzes. In current literature assessment, students are most frequently asked to apply not their knowledge of texts but procedural knowledge of how to interpret texts directly to a new situation. The interpretive use—where the individual at some later point uses what has been learned in order to come to a conceptual understanding of a phenomenon that may or may not be directly related to the item learned—can be seen in the ways by which a reader is expected to use knowledge about the legend of Pandora in constructing a brief article containing an allusion to that story or knowledge about Jacob and Esau in construing Katherine Paterson's novel *Jacob Have I Loved*. The associative use of learning is seen when something in the new phenomenon elicits an indirect connection with an item previously learned. This sort of learning is displayed in reading and response to literature, when the reader makes a connection between the story of *Hamlet* and that of *Oedipus Rex*. No explicit connection exists, but for the reader steeped in Greek drama, the implicit connections are present. So too such connections as that between Nikki Giovanni's "Nikki-Rosa" and Ben Franklin's *Autobiography,* or many other sets of works as discussed by critical readers.

There are many ways in which students can show they have used their learning both of their prior reading and of their preferences and habits of reading. As a result of the response-centered curriculum, students should be able to demonstrate that they have read and understood a number of texts and that they have deepened their ways of reading and thinking about what they have read. They should also have acquired a sense of openness to other ways of reading and alternative kinds of literature. They should be well-tempered readers.

How Do You Prove it to Them and to Their Parents and the School Administrators?

Not with the standardized reading test that is so popular. That does not catch the uses of learning except of how to read literally.

Not with a test of names, labels, and dates. That catches the replicative use of knowledge but it does not catch the practice or preference.

Not with an essay about what they have already read. That catches the replicative and it might measure the ability to generalize across texts, but it is likely to be a regurgitation of the class.

No. In order to measure across the domain and to tap the uses of learning fully, we have to focus on students reading and expressing a response to a new text.

Thus, we can say that achievement in the curriculum is defined as facility and sureness of response to the next selection the student is exposed to.

> A student has learned to bat if she makes a hit her next time up, not if she remembers how the pitcher looked the last time or what the coach told her.
>
> A student has mastered the process of responding if he responds surely and easily to a new selection, not if he remembers the teacher's lecture on the last selection.

We prove we can do by doing, not by remembering what we did. If we prove we can do by doing, the teacher's job is not to devise tests on past performance but to observe and evaluate present performance.

When we look at present performance, we must observe two things.

How well students do what we want them to do.

Whether they will do what we want them to do when they're left to their own devices.

After all, if you get students to read T.S. Eliot very carefully, finding all the paradoxes and ambiguities and relating them to the mythographic background, but they don't ever read a poem or story again, have you succeeded?

If you get people to read a lot of poetry and go to plays but do so without being able to do much more than grunt, "I like it," have you succeeded?

We want both competence and interest. If we want both, we have to measure our success both ways. We have to see whether students will and whether students can.

Tools for Seeing Whether They Will

1. A class.
2. An observer—the teacher, a teacher's aide, a supervisor, some students.
3. A means of recording what is seen—a videotape or audio tape recording of the class (useful but not necessary).
4. A checklist for recording what is done.

It might simply be a class roster that has a blank after each name for notes about who did what.

It may be a form showing not only who did what but with whom they did it, like Figure 11.1.

These aren't easy tools to use; it takes practice, but no more practice than it takes to write a good multiple-choice test.

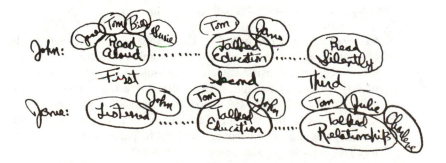

Figure 11.1

Once you have them down, you can demonstrate what students will do in class. You have shown that students engage in many kinds of articulating. They are engaged readers.

They have learned to take responsibility for their responses and to share them. They don't need you.

Seeing Whether They Will

If, on the first day with a new class, you walk in, give your students ten selections, and say, "Each of you do what he or she wants to do by way of responding to one selection," odds are that many will want to know what sort of a response you want. They may do nothing that first time.

If you walk into class the last week of a year spent with a class, give them ten selections, and say, "Each of you do what he or she wants to do by way of responding to one selection," odds are that all will do something, but that you cannot fully predict who will do what, and several will respond in ways that might offend you deep down.

They have learned to express their responses freely.

If they show each other what they do, many will comment on the other's responses, and there will be a lively exchange.

They have learned to respect each other's responses and to value their own. They might even show they have learned to generalize, to evaluate, to interpret, to envision.

Tools for Seeing if They Can
1. A class.
2. Some selections and some questions—"Which is better?" "What do these have in common?" "What significance do you find in each of them?" "Make a collage representing your impression of one."
3. A means for students to respond: paper and pencil, a tape recorder, a videotape, film, pictures for collage-making.
4. Some criteria to judge by.
   a. **Re-creating ("performing")**: Does the student appear to be translating into speech, writing, pantomime, pictures, or some other medium a consistent view of the selection, author, character, mood, action, or meaning? Does the re-creation make sense in terms of the selection. (Is it possible? plausible? probable?)
   b. **Valuing**: Does the student state his or her values clearly and honestly? Is the student simply seeking to please the group or the teacher, or is he or she being independent?
   c. **Generalizing**: Does the student display an awareness of the relationship between examples and generalizations? Does he or she

avoid the hasty generalization? Does the student go too far the other way and never risk a generalization? Is the student aware of the tentativeness of generalizations? Does he or she distinguish between generalizations and prejudices?

d. **Evaluating:** In stating an evaluation of a selection or of a response, does the student establish criteria and then match the selection or the response to the criteria? Or, does the student simply say, "It's good because, well–I liked it"?

e. **Interpreting:** Does the student make explicit the context of his or her interpretation? (Does the student specify that he or she is looking at a selection from a social rather than a psychological point of view, for example?) Does the student relate as many facets of the selection as possible to the interpretation?

f. **Analyzing:** Does the student show the points of commonality between two selections? Does he or she show the relationship between parts and whole? Does the student avoid the trap of confusing relationship and identity? Does the student note the relationship between seemingly opposed responses to a selection?

g. **Describing the envisionment:** Does the student make a verifiable description of the work as he or she envisions it? Does the description need more precision or expansion?

h. **Personalizing:** Does the student make clear the impact of the work? Does the student relate it to his or her life, his or her world? Do the student's connections ring true?

Seeing If They Can

When we seek to find out whether students will, we cast a net and see what we catch; when we seek to find out if they can, we ask them to hit a target we set up, or we look at what they do and judge them not on whether they do what we want but whether they do what they want well.

In that case, we use a criterion, some explication of a good performance. Oh, it does not have to be a rigid definition. After all, we use a lot of criteria when we determine a good meal or a good film; we should be as flexible in judging a student's paper, collage, or improvisation.

There is no reason to make our criterion that which we apply to an essay by a famous critic or a performance by a theatrical group, or even an exquisitely done collage. We can, for instance, do little better than have a recorded class discussion of a selection.

Choose one or two selections that you might think are difficult for the students, give them to half the class, and let them talk. Make notes or, better, use an audio tape or videotape recorder.

As you listen to the class or the recording, make notes about where you think the students might have checked something, where you think a student did a particularly good job picking up on somebody else's ideas, where you can suggest another example, and so forth.

Play back the tape and hand out your "marking" of the discussion. You might also invite the rest of the class to comment. They might pick up places where people were arguing from different premises, or when a person scored a really fine point.

Seeing whether they will and seeing whether they can—both are forms of evaluation—rests not on finding out what students remember in a passive way but on what processes of thinking, feeling, responding, and imagining they can bring to bear on a new experience.

Both forms of evaluation depend less on the teacher's making up a test than on the teacher establishing a situation and observing what, in fact, the students do.

Like the curriculum itself, the assessment depends on performance and process. It measures the length of the quills without annoying the porcupine.

That's Very Fine, But There Are All These National Tests

Most of those national tests measure a student's ability to use words, to read unfamiliar texts, and to make inferences. All we have set forth should lead to mastery of that kind of test, bad as it may be, and should do so better than a curriculum that is geared to recall, recognition, and application alone.

Besides, the curriculum we advocate seeks to avoid the trap into which earlier curricula fell. In the past, education in literature spent so much time being scientific, being historical, being something else, that it neglected the fact that literature is written for enjoyment and instruction, that it is intended to be read and responded to, not to have term papers written about it or to be the subject of a recitation.

In one school a teacher asked twenty-three questions on *Macbeth* in fifteen minutes, questions like *What does this word mean? What does the next line mean?* After class she was asked whether the students liked the play. "I don't know; I haven't time," she responded.

If a curriculum pays attention only to recitation and term papers about literature, the students may learn to dislike literature, and English, and school, and the mind.

"You've murdered *Hamlet* and *Macbeth*. What more do you want? My Blood?" wrote a student on a national examination.

Literature and the arts exist in the curriculum as a means for students to learn to express their emotions, their thoughts, and their imaginations as they enter into the experiences of the works they read and transliterate those experiences into film, talk, silence, writing, drama, pictures, or the like.

Literature and the arts in the curriculum can both free the imagination and help people order their worlds.

This function is served by no other part of the curriculum.

Without freedom of the imagination and personal order there can come a repressive or a revolutionary society.

It might even plug up the hole in the ozone layer.

Such runs the most pragmatic defense of the curriculium we have suggested. It is a curriculum designed to promote individuality, to promote understanding, to promote the imaginative capacity in all parts of our society.

A Series of Notes on Sources
WHERE to find "it"
and WHAT to look for

What follows is a number of pieces that we have used and found useful. Some are old, some are new. We've probably missed a lot as well. Let us begin with Perennial Sources:

The New York Times Book Review
Paperback Books in Print
The Drama Review
English Journal
Language Arts
College English
Hornbook
The New York Review of Books
The Journal of Reading
Poetry
Reader
The American Poetry Archives

Chapter 1: Lighght and Lit

Abrahamson, Richard F., and Betty Carter, eds. *Books for You: A Booklist for Senior High School Students*. Urbana, Ill.: National Council of Teachers of English, 1988.
Atwan, Robert and Harvey Wiener, eds. *Enjoying Stories*. New York: Longman, 1987.

Barrier, Michael, and Martin Williams, eds. *A Smithsonian Book of Comic-Book Comics*. Washington, D.C.: Smithsonian Institution Press, 1981.

Fader, Daniel N., and Elton MacNeill. *Hooked on Books: Program and Proof*. Los Angeles: Berkeley Publishing, 1969.

Guriand, Felix. *Larousse Encyclopaedia of Mythology*. London: Paul Hamlyn, 1959.

Hall, Stuart, and Paddy Whannel. *The Popular Arts*. New York: Pantheon, 1964.

Smith, Ron. *Mythologies of the World: A Guide to Sources*. Urbana, Ill.: National Council of Teachers of English, 1975.

Stanford, Barbara Dodds, and Karima Amin. *Black Literature for High School Students*. Urbana, Ill.: National Council of Teachers of English, 1978.

Townsend, John Rowe. *Written for Children: An Outline of English Language Children's Literature*, 2nd ed. Philadelphia: J.B. Lippincott, 1983.

White, David M., and Robert H. Abel, eds. *The Funnies: An American Idiom*. New York: Free Press, 1963.

Chapter 2: Those Kids—Readers, Writers, Listeners, Mall Rats

Applebee, Arthur N. *The Child's Concept of Story: Ages Two to Seventeen*. Chicago: University of Chicago Press, 1978.

Atwell, Nancie. *In the Middle: Writing, Reading and Learning with Adolescents*. Upper Montclair, N.J.: Boynton/Cook, 1987.

Barr, Mary, Pat D'Arcy, and Mary K. Healy. *What's Going On: Language/Learning Episodes in British and American Classrooms, Grades 4–13*. Portsmouth, N.H.: Heinemann, 1988.

Brannon, Lil, and C.H. Knoblauch. "On Students' Rights to Their Own Texts: A Model of Teacher Response." *College Composition and Communication* 33 (1982):157–166.

Britton, James, Tony Burgess, Nancy Martin, Alex McLeod, and Harold Rosen. *The Development of Writing Abilities (11–18)*. London: Macmillan, 1975.

Hazard, Paul. *Books, Children and Men*. Translated by Marguerite Mitchell. Boston: The Horn Book Company, 1944.

Hunt, Kellog J. *Grammatical Structures Written at Three Grade Levels*. Urbana, Ill.: National Council of Teachers of English, 1965.

Hynds, Susan. "International Cognitive Complexity and the Literary Response Processes of Adolescent Readers." *Research in the Teaching of English* 19 (1985):386–404.

Judy, Stephen. "The Experiential Approach: Inner Worlds to Outer Worlds." In *Eight Approaches to Teaching Composition*, edited by Timothy R. Donovan and Ben W. McClelland. Urbana, Ill.: National Council of Teachers of English, 1980.

Kohlberg, Lawrence, and Carol Gilligan. "The Adolescent as Philosopher: The Discovery of the Self in a Post-Conventional World." *Daedalus* 100 (1971):1057.

Loevinger, Jane. *Ego Development: Conceptions and Theories*. San Francisco, Jossey-Bass, 1976.

Probst, Robert. *Response and Analysis: Teaching Literature in Junior and Senior High School*. Upper Montclair, N.J.: Boynton/Cook, 1988.

Romano, Tom. *Clearing the Way: Working with Teenage Writers*. Portsmouth, N.H.: Heinemann, 1987.

Vygotsky, Lev S. *Mind in Society: The Development of Higher Psychological Processes*. Edited by M. Cole, V. John-Steiner, S. Scribner, and E. Souberman. Cambridge: Harvard University Press, 1978.

Chapter 3: Being a Chapter That Deals in Literary Theory and Its Relation to the Curriculum

Applebee, Arthur N. "Studies in the Spectator Role: An Approach to Response to Literature." In *Researching Response to Literature and the Teaching of Literature: Points of Departure*, edited by Charles R. Cooper. Norwood, N.J.: Ablex, 1985, 87–102.

Bleich, David. *Subjective Criticism*. Baltimore: Johns Hopkins University Press, 1987.

Eagleton, Terry. *Literary Theory: An Introduction*. Minneapolis: University of Minnesota Press, 1983.

Frye, Northrop. *The Educated Imagination*. Bloomington: Indiana University Press, 1964.

Griffith, Peter. *Literary Theory and English Teaching*. Philadelphia: Open University Press, 1987.

Hirsch, Eric D. *Cultural Literacy: What Every American Should Know*. New York: Vintage Books, 1987.

Holbrook, David. *English for the Rejected*. Cambridge: Cambridge University Press, 1965.

Iser, Wolfgang. *The Act of Reading*. Baltimore: Johns Hopkins University Press, 1978.

Purves, Alan C. "You Can't Teach Hamlet, He's Dead." *English Journal*, 57 (1968):832–836.

Purves, Alan C., and William C. Purves. "Cultures, Text Models and the Activity of Writing." *Research in the Teaching of English* 20 (1986):174–197.

Richards, Ivor A. *Principles of Literary Criticism*. London, Routledge, 1924.

Richards, Ivor A. *Practical Criticism: A Study of Literary Judgment*. New York: Harcourt Brace Jovanovich, 1929.

Rosenblatt, Louise M. *Literature as Exploration*. New York: Noble and Noble, 1968.

Rosenblatt, Louise M. *The Reader, The Text, The Poem: The Transactional Theory of the Literary Work*. Carbondale: Southern Illinois University Press, 1978.

Rosenthal, Robert, and Lenore Jacobson. *Pygmalion in the Classroom*. New York: Holt, Rinehart & Winston, 1968.

Said, Edward. *The World, the Text and the Critic*. Cambridge: Harvard University Press, 1983.

Scholes, Robert. *Textual Power: Literary Theory and the Teaching of English*. New Haven: Yale University Press, 1986.

Squire, James R. *The Response Processes of Adolescents While Reading Four Short Stories* (Research Report No. 2). Urbana, Ill.: National Council of Teachers of English, 1964.

Squire, James R., ed. *Response to Literature*. Urbana, Ill.: National Council of Teachers of English, 1968.

Tompkins, Jane P., ed. *Reader-Response Criticism: From Formalism to Post-Structuralism*. Baltimore: Johns Hopkins University Press, 1980.

White, E. M. "Post-structuralist Literary Criticism and the Response to Student Writing." *College Composition and Communication* 35 (1984):186–195.

Chapters 4 and 5: Enter (Stage Right) The Response-Centered Curriculum and Who's the Guide?

Benton, Michael, and Geoff Fox. *Teaching Literature: Nine to Fourteen*. London: Oxford University Press, 1985.

Bleich, David. *Readings and Feelings: An Introduction to Subjective Criticism*. Urbana, Ill.: National Council of Teachers of English, 1975.

Bruner, Jerome S. *Actual Minds, Possible Worlds*. Cambridge: Harvard University Press, 1987.

Eeds, Maryann, and Deborah Wells. "Grand Conversations: An Exploration of Meaning Construction in Literature Study Groups." *Research in the Teaching of English* 23 (1989):4–29.

Fish, Stanley. *Is There a Text in This Class? The Authority of Interpretive Communities*. Cambridge: Harvard University Press, 1980.

Koch, Kenneth. *Rose Where Did You Get That Red? Teaching Great Poetry to Children*. New York: Random House, 1974.

Mandel, Barrett J., Jr., ed. *Three Language Arts Curriculum Models: Pre-Kindergarten Through College*. Urbana, Ill.: National Council of Teachers of English, 1980.

Moffet, James, and Betty J. Wagner. *A Student-Centered Language Arts Curriculum, Grades K–13*, 3rd ed. Boston: Houghton Mifflin, 1983.

Murison-Travers, D. Molly. "The Poetry Teacher: Behaviour and Attitudes." *Research in the Teaching of English* 18 (1984):367–385.

Nelms, Ben, ed. *Literature in the Classroom: Readers, Texts and Contexts*. Urbana, Ill.: National Council of Teachers of English, 1988.

Onore, Cynthia. "The Student, the Teacher, and the Text: Negotiating Meanings Through Response and Revision." In *Writing and Response: Theory, Practice and Research*, edited by Chris Anson. Urbana, Ill.: National Council of Teachers of English, 1989.

Purves, Alan C. "The Teacher as Reader: An Anatomy." *College English* 46 (1984):259–265.

Somers, Albert B., and Janet E. Worthington. *Response Guide for Teaching Children's Books*. Urbana, Ill.: National Council of Teachers of English, 1983.

Chapter 6: "Shut Up!" He Explained: Toward A Response-Centered Community

A Language for Life (The Bullock Report). London: HMSO, 1975.

Atwell, Nancie. *In the Middle: Writing, Reading and Learning with Adolescents*. Upper Montclair, N.J.: Boynton/Cook, 1987.

Barnes, Douglas. *From Communication to Curriculum*. New York: Penguin, 1976.

Barnes, Douglas, James Britton, and Harold Rosen. *Language, the Learner, and the School*. New York: Penguin, 1970.

Bleich, David. *Readings and Feelings: An Introduction to Subjective Criticism*. Urbana, Ill.: National Council of Teachers of English, 1975.

Edwards, Anthony D., and David P.G. Westgate. *Investigating Classroom Talk*. London: The Falmer Press, 1967.

Edwards, Anthony D., and Vera J. Furlong. *The Language of Teaching*. London: Heinemann, 1978.

Fish, Stanley. *Is There a Text in This Class? The Authority of Interpretive Communities*. Cambridge: Harvard University Press, 1980.

Hynds, Susan, and Donald Rubin. *Perspectives on Talk and Learning*. Urbana, Ill.: National Council of Teachers of English, 1990.

Stafford, William. *Writing the Australian Crawl; Views on the Writer's Vocation*. Ann Arbor: University of Michigan Press, 1978.

Chapter 7: Responding Through Visual Symbols

Cole, Michael, and Helen Keysser. "The Concept of Literacy in Print and Film." In *Literacy, Language and Learning: The Nature and Consequences of Reading and Writing*, edited by David R. Olson, Nancy Torrance, and Angela Hildyard. Cambridge: Cambridge University Press, 1985, 50–72.

Eisner, Eliot. *Cognition and Curriculum*. New York: Longman, 1982.

Johnson, Terry P., and R. Louis Daphne. *Literacy Through Literature*. Portsmouth, N.H.: Heinemann, 1988.

McKowen, Clark, and William Sparke. *It's Only a Movie*. Englewood Cliffs, N.J.: Prentice-Hall, 1971.

O'Neill, Cecily, and Alan Lambert. *Drama Structures: A Practical Handbook for Teachers*. Portsmouth, N.H.: Heinemann, 1982.

Paley, Nicholas. "Kids of Survival: Experiments in the Study of Literature." *English Journal* 77 (1988):54–58.

Pierce, C.S. *Collected Papers*. Cambridge, Mass.: Cambridge University Press.

Schindel, Morton. "Confessions of a Book Fiend." *School Library Journal* 13 (1967):44–45.

Sohn, David A. *Film, the Creative Eye*. New York: George A. Pflaum, 1970.

Chapter 8: Dramatic Response and Oral Interpretation

Bolton, Gavin. "Changes in Thinking About Education." *Theory Into Practice* 24 (1985):151–156. (Entire issue is devoted to drama in education.)

Bolton, Gavin. *Toward a Theory of Drama in Education*. London: Longman, 1979.

Booth, David. *Drama Words*. Toronto: Board of Education Language Study Center, 1987.

Booth, David. "Talking in Role, Thinking for Life." *Drama Contact* No. 12 (Autumn 1988):6–11.

Byron, Ken. Drama in the English Classroom. London: Methuen, 1986.

Johnson, Liz, and Cecily O'Neill. *Dorothy Heathcote: Collected Writings on Educa-*

tion and Drama. London: Hutchinson, 1984.

Language Arts 65 (1988) No. 1: Special issue on drama.

Morgan, Norah, and Juliana Saxton. *Teaching Drama*. London: Hutchinson, 1987.

O'Neill, Cecily, and Alan Lambert. *Drama Structures: A Practical Handbook for Teachers*. Portsmouth, N.H.: Heinemann, 1982.

O'Neill, Cecily, Alan Lambert, Rosemarie Cineell, and Janet Warrwood. *Drama Guidelines*. London: Heinemann, 1977.

Theory Into Practice 24 (Summer 1985). Special issue on educating through drama.

Wagner, Betty Jane. *Dorothy Heathcote: Drama as a Learning Medium*. London: Hutchinson, 1979.

Chapter 9: Literature in the Chips

Jonassen, David H. "Hypertext Principles for Text and Courseware Design." *Educational Psychologist* 21 (1986):269–292.

Nelson, Theodor H. *Dream Machines*. South Bend, Ind.: The Distributors, 1974.

Nelson, Theodor H. *Literary Machines*. (Available from T. H. Nelson, Box 128, Swarthmore, PA 19081), 1981.

Papert, Seymour. *Mindstorms: Children, Computers and Powerful Ideas*. New York: Basic Books, 1980.

Tchudi, Stephen. "Invisible Thinking and the Hypertext." *English Journal* (January 1988): 22–30.

Troutner, Joanne. "Computers and Writers: Software and Other Resources." *English Journal* 77 (1988):92–94.

Chapter 10: But What About Writing and All That Stuff You've Been Feeding Us All These Years?

Alexander, Lloyd. "An Interview." *Language Arts* 61 (1984):411–413.

Anson, Chris M., ed. *Writing and Response: Theory, Practice, and Research*. Urbana, Ill.: National Council of Teachers of English, 1989.

Atwell, Nancie. *In the Middle: Writing, Learning and Reading with Adolescents*. Upper Montclair, N.J.: Boynton/Cook, 1987.

Britton, James, Tony Burgess, Nancy Martin, Alex McLeod, and Harold Rosen. *The Development of Writing Abilities (11–18)*. London: Macmillan, 1975.

Bruner, Jerome S. *Beyond the Information Given: Studies in the Psychology of Knowing*. Edited by J.M. Anglin. New York: W.W. Norton, 1973.

Bunge, Nancy. *Finding the Words: Conversations with Writers Who Teach*. Athens: Ohio University Press, 1985.

Donovan, Timothy, and Ben W. McClelland. *Eight Approaches to Teaching Composition*. Urbana, Ill.: National Council of Teachers of English, 1971.

Emig, Janet. *The Composing Processes of Twelfth Graders* (Research Report 13). Urbana, Ill.: National Council of Teachers of English, 1971.

Emig, Janet. *The Web of Meaning: Essays on Writing, Teaching, Learning and Thinking*. Upper Montclair, N.J.: Boynton/Cook, 1983.

Flower, Linda S., and John R. Hayes. "Images, Plans and Prose: The Representation of Meaning in Writing." *Written Communication* 1 (1984):120–160.

Freedman, Sarah W. *The Acquisition of Written Language: Response and Revision.* Norwood, N.J.: Ablex, 1985.

Gere Anne, Ruggles. ed. *Writing Across the Disciplines.* Urbana, Ill.: National Council of Teachers of English, 1985.

Gurko, Leo. *Joseph Conrad: Giant in Exile.* New York: Collier Macmillan, 1979.

Langer, Susan. *Mind: An Essay on Human Feeling.* Vol. 1. Baltimore: Johns Hopkins University Press, 1967.

Marshall, James D. "The Effects of Writing on Students' Understanding of Literary Texts." *Research in the Teaching of English* 21 (1987):30–63.

Murray, Donald. *Learning by Teaching: Selected Articles on Writing and Teaching.* Upper Montclair, N.J.: Boynton/Cook, 1982.

Purves, Alan, and Victoria Rippere. *The Elements of Writing About a Literary Work.* Urbana, Ill.: National Council of Teachers of English, 1968.

Chapters 10½ and 11: A Note on Giving Assignments and Feedback and How Can a Poor Little Literature Program Survive in That Great Big World of Tests?

Bloom, Benjamin S., Thomas Hastings, and George Madaus. *Handbook of Formation and Summative Evaluation of Student Learning.* New York: McGraw-Hill, 1971.

Cooper, Charles R. *Measuring Growth in Appreciation of Literature.* International Reading Association, 1972.

Cooper, Charles R., ed. *On the Nature and Measurement of Competency in English.* Urbana, Ill.: National Council of Teachers of English, 1981.

Elbow, Peter. *Writing Without Teachers.* New York: Oxford University Press, 1973.

Evans, Peter, ed. *Directions and Misdirections in English Evaluation.* Ottawa: Canadian Council of Teachers of English, 1985.

Fagan, William T., Julie M. Jensen, and Charles R. Cooper, eds. *Measures for Research and Evaluation in the English Language Arts.* Vols. 1 and 2. Urbana, Ill.: National Council of Teachers of English, 1975, 1985.

Fillion, Bryant. "Reading as Inquiry: An Approach to Literature Learning." *English Journal* (January 1981):39–45.

Holland, Norman. *Five Readers Reading.* New Haven: Yale University Press, 1975.

Johnston, Brian. *Assessing English: Helping Students to Reflect on Their Work.* Milton Keynes: Open University Press, 1983.

Johnston, Peter. "Process Assessment in the Language Arts." In *The Dynamics of Language Learning,* edited by James Squire. Urbana, Ill.: National Council of Teachers in English, 1987.

Loban, Walter. "Language Development and Its Evaluation." In *Reviews of Selected Published Tests in English,* edited by Alfred H. Grommon. Urbana, Ill.: National Council of Teachers of English, 1976.

Miall, David. "A Repertory Guide Study of a Poem." *Research in the Teaching of English* 19 (1985):254–268.

O'Dell, Lee, and Charles R. Cooper. "Describing Responses to Works of Fiction." *Research in the Teaching of English* 10 (1976):203–225.

Purves, Alan C. "Evaluation of Learning in Literature." *Evaluation in Education: An International Review Series* 3 (1979):93–172.

Purves, Alan, Anna Soter, Sauli Takala, and Anneli Vahapassi. "Towards a Domain-Referenced System for Classifying Composition Assignments." *Research in the Teaching of English* 18 (1984):385–416.

Searle, Dennis, and Margaret Stevenson. "Alternative Assessment Program in Language Arts." *Language Arts* 64 (1987)3:278–284.

PREPOSTEROUS

by Fredric Brown

MR. WEATHERWAX BUTTERED HIS TOAST carefully. His voice was firm. "My dear," he said, "I want it definitely understood that there shall be no more trashy reading around this apartment."

"Yes, Jason. I did not know—"

"Of course you didn't. But it is your *responsibility* to know what our son reads."

"I shall watch more closely, Jason. I did not see the magazine when he brought it in. I did not know it was here."

"Nor would I have known had I not, after I came in last night, accidentally happened to displace one of the pillows on the sofa. The periodical was hidden under it, and of course I glanced through it."

The points of Mr. Weatherwax's mustache quivered with indignation. "Such utterly ridiculous concepts, such impossibly wild ideas. *Astounding Stories*, indeed!"

He took a sip of his coffee to calm himself.

"Such inane and utterly preposterous tripe," he said. "Travel to other galaxies by means of space warps, whatever they are. Time machines, teleportation, and telekinesis. Balderdash, sheer balderdash."

"My dear Jason," said his wife, this time with just the faintest touch of asperity, "I assure you I shall watch Gerald's reading closely hereafter. I fully agree with you."

"Thank you, my dear," Mr. Weatherwax said, more kindly. "The minds of the young should not be poisoned by such wild imaginings."

He glanced at his watch and rose hastily, kissed his wife and left.

Outside the apartment door he stepped into the antigravity shaft and floated gently down two hundred-odd floors to street level where he was lucky enough to catch an atomcab immediately. "Moonport," he snapped to the robot driver, and then sat back and closed his eyes to catch the telepathecast. He'd hoped to catch a bulletin on the Fourth Martian War but it was only another routine report from Immortality Center, so he quirtled.

Index

CREDITS

Dave Morice, "288," in *Poetry Comics*. New York: Simon & Schuster. Copyright © 1982 by Dave Morice. Reprinted by permission of Simon & Schuster, Inc.

Aram Saroyan, "Lighght," in *Anthology of Concretism*. Athens, OH: The Swallow Press, 1969.

Joyce Carol Oates, "Waiting on Elvis, 1956." in *Poetry*, October-November 1987. Copyright 1987 by The Modern Poetry Association.

Roger McGough, "Goodbat Nightman," in *Modern Poets 10*. Penguin Books Ltd. Reprinted by permission of the Peters, Fraser & Dunlop Group Ltd.

"Dietician" from "Hospital Signs We'd Like to See," from *The Fall to MAD Special*. Copyright © 1970 Mad Magazine. Reprinted by permission of E.C. Publications, Inc.

Vaclev Havel, "Estrangement," in *An Anthology of Concrete Poetry*, edited by Emmett Williams, copyright © 1967, by Something Else Press. Used by permission of Rowohlt Verlag, Hamburg, West Germany.

"A Helping Hand," from SELECTED POEMS by Miroslav Holub, translated by Ian Miller and George Theiner. Penguin Books, 1967. Copyright © Miroslav Holub, 1967, translation copyright © Penguin Books Ltd. 1967.

"Twelve Rooftops Leaping," from *The Inner City Mother Goose,* by Eve Merriam. Copyright © 1969, 1982 by Eve Merriam. Reprinted by permission of Marian Reiner for the author.

Ruth Krauss, "Pineapple Play," in *The Cantilever Rainbow*. Panther Books. Copyright © 1963, 1964, 1965, by Ruth Krauss.

Reprinted from DREAMTIGERS by Jorge Luis Broges by permission of the University of Texas Press.

May Swenson, "The Wave," in HOW EVERYTHING HAPPENS. Random House.

Edgar Lee Masters, "Theodore Help God," in SPOON RIVER ANTHOLOGY. New York: Macmillan Publishing. Reprinted by permission of Morton Leavy.

Anna Maria Matute, *The Sea*. Los Ninos Tontos, Spain.

Nikki Giovanni, "Nikki-Rosa," in *Black Feeling Black Talk Black Judgement*. Copyright 1968–1970. New York: William Morrow. Reprinted by permission of William Morrow & Co.

Harper Lee, *To Kill A Mockingbird* by Harper Lee. Copyright 1960 J.B. Lippincott, 1982 Warner Books (subsidiary of Harper & Row).

From THE HOBBIT by J.R.R. Tolkien. Copyright © 1966 by J.R.R. Tolkien. Reprinted by permission of Houghton Mifflin Company.

Will Eisner, *Comics and Sequential Art*. Tamarac, FL: Poorhouse Press, 1985. Reprinted by permission of the publisher.

"Dream Variations," by Langston Hughes. New York: Random House.

"The Phoenix," from I AM PHOENIX by Paul Fleischman. Copyright © 1985 by Paul Fleischman. Text Only. Reprinted by permission of Harper & Row Publishers, Inc.